D0673213

g
e
d

DATE DUE

"Thought provoking and inspiring! A must-read for all Christians interested in stewarding God's creation."

Susan F. Drake
U.S. negotiator/delegate at
the 1992 Earth Summit

Healing the Land

A Supernatural View of Ecology

Winkie Pratney

Chosen Books
A Division of Baker Book House
Grand Rapids, Michigan 49516

© 1993 by Winkie Pratney

Published by Chosen Books
a division of Baker Book House Company
P.O. Box 6287, Grand Rapids, MI 49516-6287

Second printing, September 1994

Printed in the United States of America

Library of Congress Cataloging-in-Publication Data

Pratney, Winkie, 1944–
    Healing the land : a supernatural view of ecology / Winkie Pratney.
        p.   cm.
    Includes bibliographical references.
    ISBN 0-8007-9210-6
    1. Human ecology—Religious aspects—Christianity. 2. Nature-Religious aspects—Christianity. I. Title.
    BT695.5.P73 1993
    261.8′362—dc20   93-25494

Unless otherwise noted, Scripture quotations are from the King James Version of the Bible.

Scripture texts identified NIV are from the HOLY BIBLE, NEW INTERNATIONAL VERSION®. NIV®. Copyright © 1973, 1978, 1984 by International Bible Society. Used by permission of Zondervan Publishing House. All rights reserved.

Scripture quotations identified RSV are from the Revised Standard Version of the Bible, copyright © 1946, 1952, 1971 by the Division of Christian Education of the National Council of the Churches of Christ in the United States of America and are used by permission. All rights reserved.

Scripture quotations identified NASB are from the New American Standard Bible, © The Lockman Foundation 1960, 1962, 1963, 1968, 1971, 1972, 1973, 1975, 1977.

Contents

Part 3 Healing the Land

Appendixes

Part 1

Earth's Place in the Universe

Earth's crammed with heaven,
And every common bush afire with God;
But only he who sees takes off his shoes—
The rest sit round it and pluck blackberries.

Elizabeth Barrett Browning

Before us the creatures fall—some diminished, some
wiped completely from the face of the Creator's canvas.
Before us is the trashed gallery of earth's Maker.

Calvin DeWitt

No rain, no mushrooms.
No God, no world.

African saying

1

Toward a
Global Vision

They paved paradise, put up a parking lot.

Joni Mitchell

Give ear, O ye heavens, and I will speak; and hear, O earth,
the words of my mouth. . . . Ascribe ye greatness unto our
God. He is the Rock, his work is perfect. . . .

Deuteronomy 32:1, 3–4

This is a scary book. It deals with something both wonderful and frightening.

If you are like me, you care what people think and hate to
be wrong. I give you this book, which deals with something easily misunderstood and caricatured, knowing that it may draw
flak from people I respect. It is an attempt to take a short, simple look at a subject really too big to cover but far too important to ignore. You may love it or you may leave it. But it is something that excites and intrigues almost everyone I talk to, and I

want to take the risk and share it with you. I also think it just might hold a key to what God is up to in our time and how we can get in on His current agenda.

I confess I am disappointed in the Western Church at the end of the twentieth century. It is God's Church, despite flaws and failures, and I am gladly part of it. As the true part of the largest present belief system on earth, it is filled with fine men and women of all nations. Many are committed and evangelical and better scholars and scientists by far than dabblers and experimenters like me will ever be.

Nevertheless, I am troubled. For all the attention we give to the important issues of our time in human history, in one area we have largely missed the boat.

There are significant exceptions to spiritual blindness. Men and women with prophetic insight and more than a little courage dare us toward areas we neither care for nor want to think about. For these "voices in the wilderness" we are grateful. But despite their visions we are still strangely silent on one subject, one great theme that will not go away. It cries out for focused care and intercessory prayer, and it may be pivotal to the next great and perhaps final awakening.

It is not new. It is as old as the Bible—indeed, as old as creation. It is the theme you pick up if you read the stories, prayers and hymns of the past. I speak of *a Christian supernatural view of our world;* in particular, our spiritual relationship to the surrounding, sustaining world of living creation.

Voices from Old

The old saints in Scripture and history spoke in artless, childlike words. Like many of us, they loved God and loved mankind. Unlike us, they also loved God's creation. They never left it out of their concern for the healing of the world.

But we are grown up now. Their songs and sermons embarrass us. We are no longer at home with the world view of what Henry Drummond called "the true children of nature."

Technopeasants with a Survival Manual

Especially is this embarrassment true in the West. More than any people in history, we have new tools and open windows to the marvels of our universe. We know better than any of our predecessors what nature really looks like. Yet with an unfolding record of wonder, we live like mere technopeasants. We have a survival manual but no music. We know how to push some of the right buttons but do not know what they mean. We are so overwhelmed, as children of a technological age, with "forests" that we have forgotten the deep truth of a tree.

God so loved the world that He gave His only Son to redeem it. Shouldn't those who follow Him know something about not only sacrifice and love but the value of our world and the significance of things not seen?

God and Nature

Christians of previous centuries, by contrast, seem more alive to the presence of God in nature. Read some early records of the men and women of God who spoke of His world. They reflect joy, wonder, a sense of rapture, even, largely missing in our time. Their biographies read like the adventures of children. Without doubt they were a little afraid, but they heard the Voice call and entered the door of the House, trembling, where the great God lives.

Contrast earlier Christian songwriting, for example, with the majority of modern hymns. Older hymns give significant attention to the creation—plant, animal and bird life—as part of God's praise. As Maltbie Babcock wrote in 1901:

> This is my Father's world,
> And to my listening ears
> All nature sings, and round me rings
> The music of the spheres.

While we might expect eras rooted more in agriculture than our own to focus more on nature, the tenor of many songs con-

11

veys a more intimate link between God's world and His worship. Mankind's creation, fall and destiny were viewed in light of the rest of creation.

Typical of this perspective are the works of Isaac Watts, the great poet and songwriter of John Wesley's era. In his "Psalm for New England," Watts, like others of his time, links human sin with ecological judgment:

> When God, provoked with daring crimes,
> Scourges the madness of the times,
> He turns their fields to barren sand
> And dries their rivers from the land.
> His word can raise the springs again
> And make the withered mountains green,
> Send show'ry blessings from the skies
> And harvests in the desert rise.[1]

An Astonishing Intervention

Such an understanding prompted the Pilgrims, when their crops failed and death by starvation seemed imminent, to turn to the Lord in repentance and prayer. In fact, this very situation led to the Pilgrims' first Thanksgiving.

The following account, written in 1647, is taken directly from Governor William Bradford's *History of the Pilgrims:*

After . . . their corn was planted, all their victuals were spent and they were only to rest on God's Providence; at night not many times knowing where to have a bit of anything next day. And so as one observed, they had need to pray that God would give them their daily bread above all people in the world. Yet they bore these wants with great patience and alacrity of spirit and that for so long a time as for the most part of 2 years. . . .

I may not omit how notwithstanding all their great pains and industry and the great hopes of a large crop the Lord seemed to blast and take away the same; and to threaten further and more sore famine to them by a great drought which continued from the third week in May till about the middle of July without any rain and with great heat (for the most part), insomuch as the corn began to wither away, though it was set with fish, the moisture whereof helped it much. Yet at length it began to languish sore and some of the drier grounds were parched like withered hay, part whereof was never recovered. Upon which they set apart a solemn day of humiliation, to seek the Lord by humble and fervent prayer in this great distress.

And He was pleased to give them a gracious and speedy answer both to their own and the Indians' admiration that lived amongst them. For all morning and the greatest part of the day it was clear weather and very hot and not a cloud or any sign of rain to be seen, yet toward evening it began to overcast, and shortly after to rain with such sweet and gentle showers as gave them cause of rejoicing and blessing God.

The rain was indeed supernatural, an answer to their earnest fasting and prayer. Bradford continued:

It came without either wind or thunder or any violence and by degrees in yet abundance as that the earth was thoroughly wet and soaked therewith. Which did so apparently revive and quicken the decayed corn and other fruits as wonderful to see and made the Indians astonished to behold; and afterwards the Lord sent them such seasonable showers, with interchange of fair warm weather as through his blessing caused a fruitful and literal harvest, to their no small comfort and rejoicing. For which mercy (in time convenient) they also set apart a day of thanksgiving.

Notice a significant observation: *The Indians were "astonished"!* They of all peoples saw themselves as the warrior-guardians of the land. They knew nature. They knew the signs of rain. They knew what would happen in the normal course of events to these visitors who had pinned all their hopes of survival on a crop that was about to be destroyed by drought.

13

But what happened "astonished" them. They knew the rain was divinely sent. They knew that, in answer to prayer, the Great Spirit Himself had intervened, saving not only the lives of the visitors but also their own. And they joined in the Thanksgiving.

Centuries have passed filled with God's mighty acts in history. We of all people, at the end of this millennium, ought to have a supernatural world vision and the wisdom to know how to implement it. The tragedy is, although we know we live in a deeply spiritual world, and although nature teems with wonder and mystery, the Church, like Cinderella with amnesia, has forgotten the original miracle that made her a real princess.

What Happened to the Wonder?

Isn't it true that much of our jaded response to the discovery of God's wonders around us is no different from that of the mere materialist and mechanist? What is the usual instruction for a Christian concerned with our world? Often at heart it is no different from the counsel of the chemical: Watch your hairspray and recycle your Coke cans.

Well and good. We must all do what we can about oil slicks, better fuel efficiency and helping to save the whales. Read books on recycling. Put a brick in your toilet and a smaller head on your shower. Compost your own garbage. Keep the roadsides clean. Do not dump your chemicals in the streams. Watch out for toxic waste in your water and plant trees like Johnny Appleseed. Implement as many ideas as you can to save the earth.

But is this all it means to care for creation? If it all boils down to the merely molecular, we are of "all men most miserable." We have nothing more to say to our hurting world. We have lost the wonder.

We Have Hid in the Bushes

This is the tragedy of the Church at the edge of the next millennium: We "see not our signs." We fail to give to a world under deep threat any real perspective on the current environmental crisis, which at heart is a moral and spiritual problem.

It is becoming obvious that the best that human technology can accomplish is severely limited. To attempt to comprehensively heal even part of nature is beyond our wisdom and power. Men and women who see and understand what is happening to our planet are now being forced in the direction of what we could call "meta-matter." Molecules are not the problem. These men and women sense that some answers lie deeper than surface reality. They know that any real and lasting answer must go beyond the physical and must somehow involve the spiritual.

"The ecology," says Faith Popcorn, futurist marketing consultant for many of the top business firms in the Western world, "is the mushroom cloud of this generation." It is the central concern of today's children and tomorrow's world leaders. This emerging generation of would-be eco-warriors will listen to anybody who genuinely loves the earth. By all that is right and holy, it should surely be someone who loves the earth as God loves it.

Yet in the hour of need, we seem to have all but abandoned the field to those who are largely still searchers. The environmental movement is building an awesome P.A. system, but the ones who should be manning both the master mixer board and the mikes are too often the "roadies" and "groupies," not the Boss and His Band.

We sing our hymns in the building we call the sanctuary, but fail to carry that worship into the world in which we live— the world of science and the arts and the ordinary disciplines of life that we in our worldly Western "wisdom" have separated from the mysteries of God.

If we survive to write the history of the Church at the edge of the twenty-first century, one thing will greatly astonish future historians:

Equipped as never before with new windows on the nature of reality, the group of people best qualified to conduct the orchestra did not even hear the music. God spoke, they heard

15

His voice in the Garden and were afraid and hid themselves. They hid in the bushes of eighteenth-century empiricism, nineteenth-century rationalism and twentieth-century monasticism. They covered their spiritual nakedness with the fig leaves of formal tradition and left the study of Eden to people better acquainted with snakes and the Tree of Knowledge than the Tree of Life.

A Supernatural View of Ecology

What message do we have for a hurting world? Isaac Watts' well-known hymn written almost three centuries ago, which has become a much-loved Christmas carol, points up the intimate link between Christ's coming, His salvation and the effects of His redemption flowing to the whole creation:

> Joy to the world! The Lord has come;
> Let earth receive her King;
> Let every heart prepare Him room,
> And heaven and nature sing.
>
> Joy to the earth! The Savior reigns;
> Let men their songs employ;
> While fields and floods, rocks, hills and plains
> Repeat the sounding joy.
>
> No more let sins and sorrows grow,
> Nor thorns infest the ground;
> *He comes to make His blessings flow*
> *Far as the curse is found.*
>
> from Psalm 98

What a contrast between this earlier worship and many of our modern works! Then it was heaven and nature that sang; today it is much more likely to be only heaven. Then the redemption of nature was bound up with that of men and women; now nature is isolated, ignored, virtually invisible.

We might call what is missing *a Christian supernatural view of nature in ecology and environment.* It has been gone so long few of us even know it is missing. To recapture what we have lost in the past two centuries of unbridled technology, we must go back to where it all began.

What is so important about our world? What is so special about the creation? Where are the roots of a true mandate to care for our planet?

Our Tour of the Universe

To answer these questions in proper perspective, we must first leave earth altogether, and we shall do so by an imaginary short tour of our immediate universe. As we better understand this awesome setting, we will appreciate the utter uniqueness of our planet, how special it is in the universe, how unlike anything else that exists.

⇥ In this first section of this book, we will look at the place in the universe of earth, the one planet God loves above all else in His creation. God has only one Son and this is the world He visited, loved and became part of.

⇥ In the second section we will see how life in all its wonders actually functions on earth, and that the original rule of nature, despite our common acceptance of "the law of the jungle," was *harmony.* We will journey briefly into a world of wonder opened up only recently to our astonished eyes and see that even "simple" creations like animals and plants are much more wonderful than most of us have ever imagined.

⇥ In the last section I will open up a window on nature, the one God actually looks through. We will examine the real tragedy of the environmental crisis and, more importantly, why technology alone cannot solve it. Then we will come back to what we can do about it. Here I hope to point out one simple but costly contribution—one within the power of each of us to make—to solving the problem of pollution in our environment.

The Bible is full of the theme of *nature* and *creation*. You can scarcely turn a page without seeing it. Yet I am sorry to say that Christians (of all people!) have hardly dealt with it at all.

Dare we say it? There really *is* an answer to the global crisis we face in our time. Something can be done when technology can do no more. I want in this simple study to look with you at our world, to encourage us to see a world more alive with the power and presence of God (despite what we have done to it) than we have ever previously dared to dream.

2

Beginnings

From a distance the world seems blue and clean
And the snow-capped mountains white.

Bette Midler, "From a Distance"

The whole difference between construction and creation is
exactly this; that a thing constructed can only be loved after
it is constructed; but a thing created is loved before it exists.

G. K. Chesterton

Ideas Have Consequences

Every once in a while someone produces a really useful study
that illustrates a simple truth: *Ideas have consequences*, and what
we believe affects the way we live.

With landmark mission surveys like David Barrett's *World
Christian Encyclopedia* and Patrick Johnstone's *Operation World*,
we now have available more facts on the spiritual and moral condition of people groups and nations than any other time in
human history.

One publication called *Target Earth*, produced cooperatively by Global Mapping and Youth With A Mission, provided a simple and visually stunning summary of many critical planetary issues that face us in our time. The collection of global facts in *Target Earth* put much of this data in graphic form, covering essential areas for understanding what is happening to life on our planet.

It is impossible to tell from an ordinary map how many people live in a particular country. The city block metaphor used in *Target Earth*, by contrast, assigned each major nation a "building size" according to its population, and analyzed it in terms of its records—things like belief systems, children, literacy, sustainable food production and arable land available.

The presentation in *Target Earth* also covered global warming, pollution, crop production and life expectancy. And it charted, significantly, the comparative record of each nation in its moral as well as physical environment: crime rate, substance abuse, homelessness, numbers of people with AIDS.

Such databases, fed continuously from a global communication network, are sometimes detailed and updated more accurately than many political or even military surveys. With them we have new tools by which we can see for the first time in history the actual consequences of our actions and ideas on a planet-wide scale.

With the big picture provided by these visual databases, you may expect some things and be astonished by others. Certain trends become increasingly clear as you assemble the evidence. This much is plain: Ideas do have consequences, and what we believe does affect the way we live.

What we believe also affects the very life of the land around us for good or evil. Morals have *ecological* consequences.

It is in this area that people who, understandably, seem otherwise concerned for our planet have done surprisingly little for it. As the early Beatles sang,

You say you want a revolution,
Well, you know, we all want to change the world.

But we might rephrase the last two lines like this:

But when we talk about getting right with God;
Don't you know that you can count most out?

There are only two ways to change the future. The first is to borrow a time-junction, capacitor-equipped, nuclear-fueled DeLorean and buzz back into the past, like Michael J. Fox, to head off mistakes made back then in light of what we know today.

But time-junction, capacitor-equipped cars are in short supply. *Back to the Future* was not only a movie trilogy; it was also, unfortunately, a fantasy. Thus, we must reluctantly rule this first option out.

The second option is both real and practical. It is to take our little lives and surrender them squarely to the purposes of the living Ruler of this planet.

The Original Mandate

I want to reintroduce you to a familiar section of Scripture. The first chapter of Genesis contains a record of earth's earliest origins and some very significant passages.

In the beginning God created the heaven and the earth. And the earth was without form, and void; and darkness was upon the face of the deep. And the Spirit of God moved upon the face of the waters. And God said, Let there be light: and there was light. And God saw the light, that it was good: and God divided the light from the darkness. And God called the light Day, and the darkness he called Night. And the evening and the morning were the first day.

Genesis 1:1–5

21

This majestic description tells us three great things: first, that our world *had a beginning*; second, that it *was made by a Person*; third, that it *is distinct from the Person who made it*.

⇥ It tells us, first, that before there was anything else, God already was. He preexisted earth. Earth is His creation. It is neither eternal nor uncreated. It is neither coequal nor coexistent. It is "wonderfully made"; He Himself is the unmade Maker of wonders.

⇥ Second, this passsage tells us something absolutely basic, a theme we will come back to again and again: *Everything real starts with God.* Before we look at the heavens and the earth, before we talk about solving problems on the ground or in the sky, we need to start with God.

⇥ Third, the creation is apart from and distinct from its Creator.

Life as a Mediate Creation

The creation account in Genesis goes on to tell us how the intricate cycles and balances of all living things began. Rather than creating everything directly, God commanded the earth and the waters, themselves His creations, to participate in the creation of even higher structural forms. He sets life in motion distinct from Himself. These living forms were given the power to grow and multiply, to recreate further distinct versions of their own kind:

> And God said, Let the earth bring forth grass, the herb yielding seed, and the fruit tree yielding fruit after his kind, whose seed is in itself, upon the earth: and it was so. And the earth brought forth grass, and herb yielding seed after his kind, and the tree yielding fruit, whose seed was in itself, after his kind: and God saw that it was good.
>
> Genesis 1:11–12

And God said, Let the waters bring forth abundantly the moving creature that hath life, and fowl that may fly above the earth in the open firmament of heaven. And God created great whales, and every living creature that moveth, which the waters brought forth abundantly, after their kind, and every winged fowl after his kind: and God saw that it was good. And God blessed them, saying, Be fruitful, and multiply, and fill the waters in the seas, and let fowl multiply in the earth (verses 20–22).

And God said, Let the earth bring forth the living creature after his kind, cattle, and creeping thing, and beast of the earth after his kind: and it was so. And God made the beast of the earth after his kind, and cattle after their kind, and every thing that creepeth upon the earth after his kind: and God saw that it was good (verses 24–25).

Notice that the creation of plant, fish, bird and animal life was not direct but "mediate." God spoke in creative command to the waters and the earth to "bring forth" life. Both earth and water, like lab tools, played a mediate role in the creation process. (This is not to say that God set up a macroevolution process, or that He walked out on His creation after He began it. God commands natural forces directly and can work creatively *in*directly. Earth and water obey Him.) We are not used to this sort of language in the West, but it is the sort of language the Bible uses throughout to describe God's rule over His creation.

Mankind as a Direct Creation

Now, however, comes an important difference in the creation process:

And God said, Let us make man in our image, after our likeness . . . (verse 26).

⤴ Notice that, with the words *Let us make man,* the triune God is involved *directly* with this life form. This is the last of His creation and its crown.

23

⭑▶ Also, mankind is made in God's image. This special sort of "making" puts man at a different level from the rest of the creation. All other living things in nature are only indirect or mediate creations, brought forth by the earth or the waters. But the phrase used of our kind of creation is *In our image, after our likeness*—God's personal touch on the dust, unlike anything else He made.

Man is thus given a unique position. Man was to be, if you like, a finite, lovely copy of his Creator. We are to find meaning and purpose in an ongoing relationship with God.

And God blessed them, and God said unto them, Be fruitful, and multiply, and replenish the earth, and subdue it: and have dominion over the fish of the sea, and over the fowl of the air, and over every living thing that moveth upon the earth (verse 28).

Think about this for a moment. Creation relates to man as man relates to his Creator. God's command to all the rest of creation—fish, birds, insects and beasts—was only to multiply. But mankind is distinct from the rest of the creation, not only in the way he is made. He got two extra responsibilities by virtue of his uniqueness: to "subdue" and to "have dominion."

Subdue and Take Dominion

Even before God's warning recorded in Genesis 2—"Of the tree of the knowledge of good and evil, thou shalt not eat"—and before any account of man's wrongdoing, he was given regency over the rest of nature, the task of care and keeping. This injunction to discipline nature preceded the appearance of evil.

Humanity is not only to be fruitful and multiply and replenish the earth, but also to "subdue" it (Genesis 1:28). You can easily find that the word *subdue* (Hebrew *kabash*, kaw-bash) means primarily to "tread down, to conquer, to subdue or bring into

24

subjection," an obvious military meaning. It has the sense of "taking authority from and asserting authority over."

License to Rape?

Here some critics have leveled charges against the Church. Some have said (as we shall discuss in chapter 4) that this command is a license for the rape and misuse of creation. It would be easy to suppose it so. Few have anything but a negative reaction to a word like *subdue*. Nor does anyone deny that the word for *subdue* used here points to the putting down of something and to the need for a strong hand, one of discipline and control.

Yet all of life demands that some things be kept in check. The prolific urge originally implanted in nature to fill and multiply has no built-in moral constraint, no inherent control, no limit. You understand this every time you cultivate a crop. Not only is it not wrong to "subdue," but when the ultimate end is to be a harvest or garden—something more beautiful and wonderful than a jungle—it is absolutely essential.

Someone somewhere has to take mediate charge of this free-wheeling, teeming and dizzy lot. All of creation looked initially like a teenager drunk with the joy of being alive. Someone had to give the show some semblance of sanity and order. No one will deny that this is still true today. In any order, even one in which we imagine absolute equality, someone has to take charge. Somebody has to mow the lawns.

Notice that the commands to "subdue" and "take dominion" are given in the context of *man made in God's image*. Critics who see only the results of a creation deeply hurt by fallen man tend to read in their own prejudices against the God of the Bible.

Things Weren't Intended This Way

Yet consider the full sweep of what God says. The very fact that we do not like what has happened in the earth tells us that things were not first made like this. We feel bad because we have departed from God's original model. But while the word *subdue* does mean to impose power or control, it does not have to mean tyranny. Though we have few examples of justice and wise limits from those placed in authority, an appointed ruler does not have to be rapacious, brutal, greedy or arbitrary in exercising authority.

Indeed, the very same word is later used of God's dealing with sin in our lives. Micah 7:18–19 sets *subdue* in the context of God's mercy and compassion: ". . . He delighteth in mercy. He will turn again, he will have compassion on us; he will subdue our iniquities; and thou wilt cast all their sins into the depths of the sea."

The other word and injunction given in Genesis 1:28 is "to have dominion" (*radah*, raw-daw). While similar in its root meaning to *subdue*, meaning to tread on or to subjugate, it also carries an accountancy sense. It has a special meaning: "to crumble off." It has a related Hebrew root, *radad*, which means not only to tread in pieces or conquer, but also to overlay or to spend. To take dominion, then, means not only to win over but to reapportion, to take where there is too much and move it somewhere else.

Nature and Man: Beauty and the Beast

Man was not only to help keep nature in check, but to be friends with and receive enjoyment from nature as his first companion in the Garden:[1]

> And the LORD God planted a garden eastward in Eden; and there he put the man whom he had formed. And out of the ground made the LORD God to grow every tree that is pleasant to the sight, and good for food. . . .
>
> Genesis 2:8–9

The plant life of the Garden was a constant source of pleasure to Adam. Right in the center of that Garden was the constant reminder of eternal life itself, the tree of life, as well as the one moral boundary (depicted also in a plant) that he must not transgress, the tree of the knowledge of good and evil.

And imagine how much fun God had making the animals! I never cease to marvel at His imagination, wisdom and outright humor. I think it was His peculiar joy to watch His greatest creation greet the rest of earth's living family filled with childlike wonder. God brought Adam the animals to see what he would name them.

> . . . And whatsoever Adam called every living creature, that was the name thereof. And Adam gave names to all cattle, and to the fowl of the air, and to every beast of the field . . . (verses 19–20).

What's in a Name?

To name anything in Hebrew, as in many other cultures throughout history, implied a profound knowledge of that creation's place in this world. It was to know precisely what that creation was and where it ultimately belonged. A name in this early world was a statement of essential nature.

Adam, with an untrammeled mind unbound by sin or its consequences, must have had a task more wonderful and fulfilling than any of us can imagine. He gave names to all the animals, and God was delighted with his delight.

Yet in all the deep knowledge of creation that this implied, on levels of communication and understanding beyond our comprehension, Adam still had no one like his own kind.

With all the beauty in the Garden, and notwithstanding Adam's relationship with the plants and trees, God saw his need for a higher level of friendship:

> And the LORD God said, It is not good that the man should be alone; I will make him an help meet for him.
>
> Genesis 2:18

27

The Fall

The rest of the sad story we all know. His highest created companion, the deepest love that transcended Adam's love for the rest of creation, fell prey to temptation and took her mate with her. Both animal and plant life (the snake and the fruit) became the vehicles of temptation, and mankind, in one terrible act, lost almost everything:

> And unto Adam [God] said, . . .Cursed is the ground for thy sake; in sorrow shalt thou eat of it all the days of thy life; thorns also and thistles shall it bring forth to thee; and thou shalt eat the herb of the field; in the sweat of thy face shalt thou eat bread, till thou return unto the ground; for out of it wast thou taken: for dust thou art, and unto dust shalt thou return.
>
> And the LORD God said, Behold, the man is become as one of us, to know good and evil: and now, lest he put forth his hand, and take also of the tree of life, and eat, and live for ever: Therefore the LORD God sent him forth from the garden of Eden, to till the ground from whence he was taken. So he drove out the man; and he placed at the east of the garden of Eden Cherubims, and a flaming sword which turned every way, to keep the way of the tree of life.
>
> Genesis 3:17–19, 22–24

Man Becomes Beast

Mankind's kingly right over the earth had been given by God, and continued even after the Fall and the flood. But, as Erich Saer points out in *The Dawn of World Redemption:*

> Now his attitude to Nature, especially in the animal world, is no longer that of original harmony, but a relationship of force, oppression and conflict. In Paradise the spiritual majesty of the earthly king had, in a certain sense, "magically" bound the animal world; but now it was a lordship with fear on the one side and timidity (or indeed paralyzing terror) on the other.[2]

Because of the Fall, we have a sad new fairy story in nature and man: Beauty and the Beast. What was once the crown of creation has become exiled, marred and dangerous. Yet Beauty still sees beyond the fallen shell and woos her fallen, bewitched Beast in hope. As Isaac Watts wrote:

> Lord, what was man when made at first,
> Adam, the offspring of the dust,
> That Thou should'st set him and his race
> But just below an angel's place?
>
> That Thou should'st raise his nature so
> And make him Lord of all below;
> Make every beast and bird submit
> And laid the fishes at his feet?

What was man, indeed! Seen only by our sorry record in history, few would place us in company with any other than the dark angels! We are Beast indeed. No wonder Beauty was afraid.

The awful consequences of that Fall we still live out today. We know, more than any generation in history, just how damaging that first selfish choice proved to be. We have much more on this damage to look at later. Before we finish, I hope to help you see more than ever before how utterly ugly sin really is.

But we will not finish there. Isaac Watts did not. This fairy tale, like all good stories, has a happy ending, as Watts' paraphrase from Psalm 8 indicates:

> . . . The world to come, redeem'd from all
> The miseries that attend the fall,
> New-made and glorious shall submit
> At our exalted Saviour's feet.

Beyond the Garden

You might know the old Woodstock dream:

> We are caught in the devil's bargain,
> And we've got to get ourselves back to the Garden.

But God isn't going back to any garden. He never goes back. The Bible record begins in a Garden, all right, but it ends in a City of Light, forever without night, with clear, gold streets like glass and a river of life flowing out from the throne of its Ruler through the midst of the Tree of Life, whose leaves are for the healing of the nations.

God started out the human story in the Garden, but He is moving forward toward a city, the final City we have always wanted to build—a glorious, harmonic wonder of technology, beauty and spirituality combined, a "holy technology" for a new race of the redeemed from every nation.

3

Glasses
on the Mind

The Roots of True Science

If you visit the Library of Congress before it is renovated beyond redemption, you will see, all around the gallery overlooking the main reading hall, alcoves dedicated to each of the major disciplines. In the alcove under *Religion* there is, naturally, a quote from the Bible:

> What doth the Lord require of thee, but to do justly, and to love mercy, and to walk humbly with thy God?

The quote under *History* is also interesting—not Scripture, but a quote from a poet who understood Scripture:

> One God, one law, one element,
> and one far-off divine event,
> to which the whole creation moves.

That, from Lord Tennyson, is quite a summary of history!

But the quote under *Science* is the mind-blowing one. Out of the millions of words stored in the Library of Congress, with all the possibilities in print of the records in technology, someone chose a quote for the science alcove who understood the roots of true science. This quote sums up the whole of observed reality in laws of matter, energy and phenomena. It, too, is a quote from the Bible:

> The heavens declare the glory of God; and the firmament showeth his handiwork.

"Day unto day uttereth speech," continued the psalmist, "and night unto night showeth knowledge. There is no speech nor language, where their voice is not heard. Their line is gone out through all the earth, and their words to the end of the world" (Psalm 19:2–4a).

When mankind lost that perspective on nature, we began to lose touch with the harmony of our world. Since scientism led to a divorce between anything supernatural and what is spoken of as scientific, our world has experienced an escalating mess.

Facts Are Not the Issue

The majority of materialists today believe that the facts of science have done away with any need for the spiritual. But facts have never been an enemy of faith. The Bible does not say, "Be ye transformed by the removal of your minds," in the nonexistent book of Hezekiah! If you wish to disprove the resurrection of Jesus Christ, you will have to deal first not with philosophy or theology but with history. A hard look at facts always helps confirm the core truth of Christianity.

But truth is not the real issue in the battleground of skepticism. The problem is rarely wrong facts, but rather wrong presuppositions—the "glasses" we wear on our minds when we look at those facts.

To illustrate this on a kid's level I draw a fish and a submarine underwater:

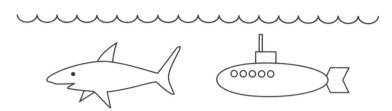

The fact is, there are similarities between these two objects, the fish and the sub. They have similar shapes, they both have light-gathering apparati, they both have tails, they both move. There is similarity. That is fact.

But now let me make an unspoken assumption:

Similarity = common ancestry

With the facts in hand and this assumption in the back of my mind, I can now point out to you, with great attention to detail, that this fish is probably a "micro-miniaturized, poly-morphic-alloyed, Terminator-2–evolved, great-great-grand-descendent of the original, clumsier and simpler form—a submarine." It is obvious, you see. The facts are there.

The problem with this odd conclusion is not the facts. The facts are obvious: The objects *are* similar. No one can argue with the facts.

But change my unspoken assumption to something else:

Similarity = common design

Now you surmise from the *same* facts a wholly different conclusion. Both fish and sub were designed to work well underwater. This is true whether we are considering fish and subs or the similar shapes of animal babies and human babies in the womb (morphology or embryology). The problem usually lies *behind* the facts—not false facts, but false premises, false assumptions. The problem is the "glasses" you wear on your mind through which you look at those facts.

Is That Really Chocolate Milk?

For some years now I have worn clip-on shades. I have tried many varieties over the decades and am now settled happily on shades they call "blue-blockers." I buy three sets for three levels of light: dark brown for snow or super-bright sunshine, mid-orange for ordinary bright sun, and yellow that can be worn during rain, fog or even at night (hunters and SWAT teams use them for shooting).

When you put on a pair of blue-blockers, they lock out not only ultraviolet glare but the high blues, a frequency our eyes have trouble focusing on easily. The world often seems sharper viewed through these shades.

I went into a cafeteria once with the yellow set on and selected what I thought was chocolate milk. When I got back to the table to drink it, it turned out to be that awful, half-a-percent skim stuff posing as milk that I cannot stand. I couldn't understand it. When I was standing in line it was chocolate milk. When I got back to the table it was changed like wine into water, in a lowfat way.

Then I realized I had gone through the line with my shades on. Since the skim milk carton is blue, and since blue-blockers knock out some blues, the carton looked brown through my glasses. Instant transformation.

What Are Your Hidden Assumptions?

So it is with our world. All of us, religious or not, have hidden presuppositions, unspoken assumptions, perception grids through which we screen all encountered reality. No one except God is exempt from these. What we have are glasses on the mind. The presuppositions or assumptions we carry with us constitute what some call our "world view." Unless corrected by continual exposure to the light of God's revealed truth, we will always see skim milk as chocolate and never know why we keep missing out.

If your premise or assumption is wrong, in other words, even if you have all the right facts and wholly correct logic, your conclusion will be wrong. **With the right facts and a false premise, you can for all the right reasons come to the wrong conclusion.** And you may never even know why you are wrong.

It is the task of truth to crack our false distorting glasses. We never know they are there until we stop seeing *through* them and begin to actually look *at* them.

God speaks to His world by His Word. His truth is the finger that first touches our unseen glasses so that we can realize, sometimes for the very first time, that we are wearing them. It takes great courage to admit that, and greater courage still to learn to live with a better, clearer pair.

One day His light will shine on each honest heart fully and all our damaged sight will be healed. We will no longer "see through a glass, darkly." We will, with a shock, see the world as it actually is and "know even as also [we are] known." In the world of truth, God takes everybody's glasses off to enable them to see reality. Reality is not pretend, not hidden, not even colored. It is simply what *is*.

A Vision of Hope in the World

Someone gave me a sweatshirt once with a beautiful picture of earth shot from space. The caption reads, *I'm not a hitchhiker, I'm a crew member.* As a crew member, I would like to start you now on the little tour I promised you in chapter 1—the imaginary tour of our immediate universe, lifting off into space to see our planet in better perspective.

The Bible proceeds on the premise that this planet is alive with the fullness of God. Consider that the prophets, even in times of great moral darkness with bad things going on, still declared that the earth is filled with the glory of God. They saw something that transcended the mess. Their different mindset gave them confidence despite the ugliness.

The Prophet and the College Kid

One of the best illustrations of this is what happened when the prophet Elisha was surrounded by Syrians in 2 Kings 6. The prophet is in his house with a kid from Bible college training with him as a "young gun" butler, and perhaps a dog. (The dog is optional.) The hordes of an enemy army come to surround this prophet and pick him up. The Bible college kid is terrified and screams something about writing home to his mother: "Please, Mr. Custer, I don't want to go."

Then the prophet says something odd to him: "Don't be afraid. There are more with us than there are with them."

Perhaps the young servant thinks he said, "There are more of us than there are of them." He counts again just to make sure: One prophet (him). One servant (me). One dog (optional). Full count: Two or three. He looks out the window: One entire army.

Nope. Most uneven odds. Prophet he may be, but he's no accountant. More of us indeed!

He looks at the prophet, and his look says it all: *I'm too young to die, and my boss has departed from reality!*

Then the prophet says, "Lord, open his eyes."

We need to take a big view of this. Here is a helicopter shot of this scene:

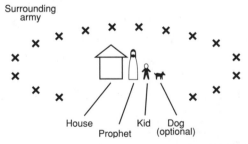

There are the house and the army surrounding the prophet and the kid. (The optional dog is probably running for the hills himself!) The kid is thinking, *I've got better eyes than you, old man. I can see those food-processor blades on the sides of their chariots. I understand this.*

36

But to "see" we need to go up even higher. So here is a spiritual satellite shot of this scene:

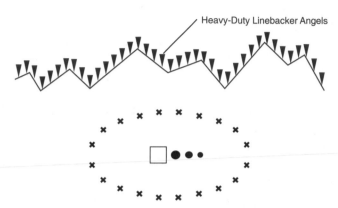

Heavy-Duty Linebacker Angels

Here is the really big picture. What the kid doesn't see is all those angels filling the hills around with drawn light sabres, waiting for one word from the prophet who sees things as they really are: "There are more with us than there are with them."

Only one-third of the angels fell. Two-thirds are still good guys. That means the majority of the universe is righteous.

Granted, we live on a fallen planet, the headquarters of the first rebellion. When hell holds a convention, they always meet on earth. From our small, persecuted perspective, things look pretty bleak at times for those who want to remain faithful to God. There are too many rebels and too few under His rule.

But remember, in the whole picture, from a higher perspective, things are different than how they seem down here.

So I want you to have a change of vision. Look at our world today through new eyes—as a world ruled by a God of greatness and creative love.

Owners of the World

Now let me draw your attention to the end of Ezekiel 44, which gives a wonderful description of the consequences of being God's true representatives:

> It shall be unto [the priests] for an inheritance: I am their
> inheritance: and ye shall give them no possession in Israel: I
> am their possession. They shall eat the meat offering, and the
> sin offering, and the trespass offering; and every dedicated
> thing in Israel shall be theirs. And the first of all the firstfruits
> of all things, and every oblation of all . . . shall be the priest's.
>
> Ezekiel 44:28–30a

In response to verse 28—"I am their inheritance . . . I am
their possession"—Charles Spurgeon commented, "When you
have Him, what more do you need?"

The World Is Yours

When you belong to God, all the world He made is yours
as well. There is no separate, sacred place you have to visit in
order to experience His presence. It all belongs to you. And those
who are truly dedicated to God own the world.

Let me offer a comparative scenario. If you walked into your
house and caught a strange kid raiding your refrigerator, you would
probably frighten him (and vice-versa). But if it was *your* child
looking in the refrigerator, he might simply say, "Hi. You want
something, too?" When it is your house, everything in it is yours.

Those whose lives are committed to serving God, according to that passage in Ezekiel, will get in first on the joys and
blessings of God. They get to share in the meat offering, the sin
offering, the trespass offering, the sacrifices made to God. All
the "dedicated things" are theirs as well. When you are owned
by Him, in other words, it is all yours, too.

> Ye shall also give unto the priest the first of your dough, that
> he may cause the blessing to rest in thine house (verse 30b).

I don't know whether this is the original mandate for taking up a collection in church, but there is a principle at work:
Those who serve God feel at home in His world.

The Choice

In Romans 8 the apostle Paul makes a clear distinction between those who serve God and those who serve the flesh:

> They that are after the flesh do mind the things of the flesh; but they that are after the Spirit the things of the Spirit. For to be carnally minded is death; but to be spiritually minded is life and peace.
>
> Romans 8:5–6

If you connect your life to selfishness, you will reap death as a consequence. But for a spiritual mind, walking according to "the law of the Spirit of life in Christ Jesus" (verse 2), the consequence is life and peace.

> I reckon that the sufferings of this present time are not worthy to be compared with the glory which shall be revealed in us. For the earnest expectation of the creature waiteth for the manifestation of the sons of God (verses 18–19).

Keeping this intriguing statement in mind (which we shall consider in chapter 9), let's see how our view of creation is altered by our "glasses on the mind."

4

Three Views
of the World

A man who cannot think of his Creator as a Being other than himself cannot be said to have a religion.

Owen Barfield

A religion without mystery must be a religion without God.

Jeremy Taylor

Looked at the wrong way, nature can be a substitute for God. This is because relative beauty can be jealous of absolute beauty.

Hubert Van Zeller

To have a valid reason to be concerned about anything in life outside your own immediate pleasure, you must have a world view, some sort of moral presupposition—the happiness of others, perhaps, or the state of the nations, or the crisis facing the environment. And among all the multiple shades of "glasses on the mind" that we juggle in the twentieth century, there are, strangely enough, only three basic ones:

☙ First, the irreverent **Western** view (hardly a moral pre-supposition at all) that *we are only chemicals* that should show no concern; that humankind and creation are wholly the product of chance, time and matter—a lucky accident we have been trying to learn to live with.

☙ Second, the ancient answer of **Eastern** philosophy that *the world itself is divine,* that all nature is one and, like us, part of God, so we should treat it and one another with reverence, even worship. This view can go in one of two directions: *pantheism*—that everything is God, or that God is the reality or principle behind everything; or *monism*—that everything except God is fantasy, or that "God" is actually the soul of nature.

☙ Third, the **biblical** view, neither Eastern nor Western, that *earth and the universe were designed with humanity as the crown of creation and utterly special.* Nature is, in this picture, neither chemical nor divine, but a supernaturally co-created gift of God that has suffered a terrible loss because of the failure and neglect of its appointed caretaker—man and woman.

Which of these world views each of us adopts will affect the material world around us for good or for evil. Since ideas do indeed have consequences, what are the results of the one we embrace as our own?

The Western View: Nature as Chemicals

Men and women have made various attempts to approach environmental problems philosophically. The irreligious West has tended to think of you or me basically as a bag of complex chemicals reacting to the environment. Here is the equation the rationalistic West has given for the past century:

Time + chance + matter = mankind and the universe

As Francis Schaeffer pointed out some years ago, time is (unless you believe in Father Time) impersonal. Chance and matter, too, are impersonal—unless you believe in the personality of hydrogen atoms. A guy from Los Angeles once sent me a sixteen-page study on the personality of a hydrogen atom. At least he was thinking!

The problem with this rationalistic equation, if true, is how three *im*personals can make a person.

A Kiss Is Just a Chemical Reaction

As a philosophy of life, this equation (which many of us were given along with our Wheaties in the morning when we were growing up) puts man into the chemical machine. If it is true, if we are all just chemicals reacting in the environment, then you as a thinking Western person would be forced to conclude, "There must be no such things as truth, beauty, moral values, right and wrong, love."

So said Bertrand Russell:

Man is the product of causes which had no prevision of the end they were achieving; . . . his origin, his growth, his hopes and fears, his loves and beliefs are but the outcome of accidental collocations of atoms. . . . No fire, no heroism, no intensity of thought and feeling can preserve an individual life beyond the grave. . . . Only within the scaffolding of these truths, only on the firm foundation of unyielding despair, can the soul's habitation henceforth be safely built.[1]

So your kissing your husband or wife, girlfriend or boyfriend, and what you feel for your child, are nothing more than a chemical reaction.

Professor B. F. Skinner took this idea to its logical end. Basically he said that the equation *is* true, that there are no such things as beauty, love or truth. Everything is just chemicals and environmental conditioning.

43

Of course, if what Dr. Skinner said is true, that there is no such thing as truth, then what he said isn't true at all! Which is a bit embarrassing, when you think about it.

There is a simple way to put the Western idea of origins:

Frog + princess kiss = handsome prince
(This is called "fairy story")

Frog + 10 billion years = handsome prince
(This is called "science")

Why Care About the Future?

If this Western picture of the world is true, then we have lost not only all moral possibility and consequences, but any philosophical reason—and certainly any theological one, if there is no God, no heaven, no life after death—to take care of our planet. There is no reason at all, other than a pragmatic one, to care: "I'm here and I hope to stay." What do chemicals care about the future, or even their children's future? When you die that's it; you go into the ground and simplify. Just chemicals again. Goodbye.

As the unknown author of "Deteriorata" (a satire on "Desiderata") put it:

> You are a fluke of the universe
> You have no right to be here
> Whether you hear it or not
> The universe is laughing behind your back.

Many people have tried bravely to live this out as if they had no personal sense of origin. But without this sense a person has no sense of destiny or meaning. Many kids come to colleges and universities feeling this sense of futility. When they ask early on, "What am I?", they are told: "A first-year student. Just study your brains out, and don't ask any real questions."

There has to be more to life than that!

An Answer for Diversity

The one claim to strength in Western thinking is its explanation of the variety we see around us. The West does have an answer for the *diversity* in the universe: Diversity comes as the result of chance, random combinations, fortunate mutations, lucky contingencies.

A Western, materialistic view of nature has an answer for difference but no real answer for the unity, law, structure, harmony we see in the universe. Think again of the Western picture of man as the product of blind, undirected chance and matter, while all around us is a universe that speaks of laws, of harmony and objects that behave according to order.

The West has no real answer for law, form, structure. Yet the universe exists with law and form and structure. Why this should be so has no real answer in the equations of chance. Nature has her rules and you try to break them at your peril.

The Eastern View: Nature as God

According to Eastern philosophy, we are one with all things and share the same essential "stuff" of Reality, which is spirit. In fact, *we are God itself.* The world around us that seems real is actually only a dream of God, a fantasy of some kind. Matter itself is false, and enjoyment of anything connected to it is untrue.

Explains A. C. Bhaktivedanta Swami Prabhupada in *The Nectar of Devotion:*

> Every living entity under the spell of material energy is held to be in an abnormal condition of madness. . . . The conditioned soul is mad because he is always engaged in activities which are the causes of bondage and suffering. . . . Spirit soul in its original condition is joyful, blissful, eternal and full of knowledge. Only by implication in material activities has he become miserable, temporary and full of ignorance.[2]

45

Sin Is Merely Ignorance

The deep problem with humanity is a bad cosmic memory. Sin is not a moral act; it is merely *ignorance of the true nature of reality.* And the reason the earth is in trouble is plain ignorance.

A "realized soul" is one who understands that the world and everything in it means nothing at all, and that it is a mistake in spiritual perception to attach value to anything connected with it. The whole of the world to an Eastern holy man is illusory, unreal, simply a dream.

We Are What We Deserve

A second idea inexorably joins this first one—the doctrine of *karma.* Based on reincarnation, it is the Eastern idea of perfect justice: *You suffer in this life the consequences of your ignorance in the last life.* You get what you deserve.

Punishment is not thus for wrong; it is for ignorance. Everything, no matter how different or opposite, is according to Eastern thought only another way of looking at the same thing. Anything in our world that we might think of as right or wrong, according to this world view, comes from ignorance (once again) of the true nature of reality.

We suffer when we do not understand our place as part of that ultimate reality we call God. Because everything in the universe has balance, we are punished for our "sins of attachment" committed in a previous life. Our punishment for this ignorance is *material existence;* we are reborn. This is our karma—to suffer in life after life the consequences of our ignorance. Hell, in Eastern thought, is to be born again—and again and again.

Our rebirths move us up and down in the scale of material existence, depending on our actions and understanding during our stay here, from plant to insect to animal to untouchable to royal prince, perhaps even to holy man. We all are given a temporary place in this illusionary world. Where we are, what we are, is what we deserve.

Vanquished means that after getting this human form of life, a person does not come out of the entanglement of birth and death and thus misses his golden opportunity. Such a person does not know where he is being thrown by the laws of nature. He will be thrown into a cycle of birth and death involving 8,400,000 species of life and his spiritual identity will remain lost. One does not know whether he is going to be a plant, or a beast, or a bird. . . .[3]

We are doomed to repeat this cycle endlessly, reincarnation after reincarnation, until finally, through some form of enlightenment, we may one day drop off this wheel of birth and rebirth into our original state as part of God.

Ah So, Grasshopper

Whatever is, then, *is right.* You may not like it; you may hurt because of it. But ultimately you must accept it. Blow it here as a man and you may come back in the next rebirth as something less than a man—a monkey, perhaps an insect.

And here is the heart of the Eastern reverence for life. It is not so much tenderness for fallen, hurting or unfortunate creation (the East has never tried to redeem its untouchables) as the belief that if you do not act wisely now, you will pay for it next time. If you do wrong in this life, you will suffer in the next one. If you hurt another, you will hurt yourself. Reverence for life is founded in the fear of karmic reprisal.

The Buddhist Scriptures teach:

The slightest act of charity, even in the lowest class of persons, such as saving the life of an insect out of pity . . . shall bring to the doer of it consequent benefit. . . . All living things of whatsoever sort call forth compassion and pity as they shall always exist in spirit.[4]

And in Hinduism:

47

He who injures animals that are not injurious, from a wish
to give himself pleasure, adds nothing to his own happiness,
living or dead; while he who gives no creature willingly the
pain of confinement or death but seeks the good of all sen-
tient beings enjoys bliss without end.[5]

Behave wisely and revere other life forms with the knowledge that at heart they, too, are vehicles for God, and you may
one day qualify to escape the wheel and leave forever the illusionary world of matter, space and time. (If you do, of course,
you will not be back to tell anyone. The very fact that a holy
man is still here is a reflection on his actual spiritual attainment.
He has not yet made it off the wheel.)

Holiness Is Stoicism

Such a religious world view may teach you to be brave in
the face of terrible circumstances, but it offers no incentive to
confront those circumstances as wrong. Although our deepest
human feelings rise up in anger against the hurts and ills of the
body, the way of a true holy man of the East has traditionally
been stoicism, accommodation and acceptance. Matter, after all,
is not important. All that counts is the spiritual world.

This is why countries that have adopted Eastern philosophy
as a mindset have struggled on a popular level with issues like
poverty, sickness and famine as spiritual problems. "What was
candy for the saint turned out to be poison for the ordinary person," said one Eastern teacher, looking back on his nation's sad
history.

Will Durant commented on India's political history:

Weakened by division it succumbed to invaders; impoverished
by invaders it lost all power of resistance and took refuge in
supernatural consolations; it argued that both mastery and
slavery were superficial delusions and concluded that freedom
of the body or the nation was hardly worth defending in so
brief a life. The bitter lesson that may be drawn from this
tragedy is that eternal vigilance is the price of civilization.[6]

An Answer for Unity

An Eastern view of the world, although it doesn't confront wrong, does provide a good answer for the unity and harmony we see all around us. It says, "Yes, we all really are one—you, me, the sky, the sea, the flea and the redwood tree."

The ancient view that "all reality is one" was shared by many people groups around the world long before it was imported to the West via the religious and philosophical movements of the previous century, as well as by the counterculture of the '60s and '70s and the New Agers of the '90s. Just as the water of the ocean is the same stuff as an individual drop separated from it, God is, according to this world view, the whole of reality. His "stuff" is essentially the same as your "stuff."

Your problem, according to the East, is that you think you are somehow distinct from the rest of creation. The way to solve that problem in Eastern thought is to lose your sense of individuality. If you are of the same stuff as God and the rest of the universe, one with all things, salvation consists in regaining that profound unity by understanding—by the conquest of illusion.

If that drop of water (small H_2O) returns to the ocean (big H_2O), it loses its individual identity and becomes swallowed up in the ocean of Reality. You lose yourself in the whole. That, to the East, is salvation. To be saved is to be individually lost! This is "Nirvana"—not the rock group, but Eastern heaven. *Nothingness.*

The Supernatural View: Nature as Gift

The Bible picture, as I said at the beginning of this chapter, is neither Eastern nor Western. It does not (like Western secularism) reduce us to mere reacting substances in a sea of chaos and chance. Nor does it (like Eastern mysticism) say that our problem is one of mere ignorance of the true nature of reality. It does not say that salvation consists in merely accepting what *is* as O.K., giving us no more vision or purpose than seeking to bring all life, in the name of God, down to the common level of the grass. And it does not require that we lose our root identity as human beings.

In absolute contrast to Eastern philosophy, the Bible does not teach that matter is bad. God *likes* matter. He created matter to bring Him glory. Matter is mysterious but a constant reminder that creation is real. Jesus came in the flesh—something demons don't like to admit. He is at the right hand of the Father with a real human body. Glorified, yes; but the fact that Jesus rose from the dead and directs His Kingdom as God in the flesh says that matter itself is wonderful.

Our relationship with the world, as Francis Schaeffer pointed out decades ago, is not that we are inherently one *with* God, but that we are creations *of* God. We bear a real relationship to nature—not that we and it are both part of God, but that we are both *co-creations.* A tree, though just a tree, has its own beauty as a tree and is to be respected as part of the creation of God. It is not one with me, not a different manifestation of God, but we share the same purpose of created reality to bring glory to God.

This is what rings true to us, of course, when we look at Eastern religions. Although the Bible teaches the exact opposite of the core ideas of Eastern thought (we are *not* the same substance as the uncreated God), we really are in a way one with the creation. We share the same "creation stuff." As His creatures, we are all upheld by His creative life and power as one dependent creation.

And because we are all creations of God, human beings are to love and care for all His creatures.

The Bible: War on Creation?

The Bible has been blamed for many things over the centuries. We have long been told that its teaching is the root of our environmental problems. Lynn White, historian at the University of California, Berkeley, wrote that Christianity not only established a dualism of man and nature, but insisted it is God's will that man exploit nature. . . . Christianity bears a huge burden of guilt.[7]

Ian L. McHarg, a Scottish ecologist and town planner as far back as 1969, called the Genesis record of man's dominion "a declaration of war on nature."[8] In his Dunning Trust lectures of 1972–1973, he angrily blamed "three horrifying lines" of the Bible record, "this ghastly, calamitous text," for what he summed up as

> one text of compounded horror which will guarantee that the relationship of man to nature can only be destruction, which will atrophy any creative skill . . . which will explain all the destruction and all the despoilation accomplished for at least these 2,000 years.[9]

The Bible: Care for Creation

Regardless of how both the Church and her enemies have ill-treated or been ignorant of the message of the Bible, one thing is certain. *The whole tenor and thrust of the Bible is toward salvation and healing,* not only of individuals, but of families, nations and countries—indeed, *of the very land itself.* The Bible demands personal responsibility on all levels of life and calls for a level of commitment to care for life unmatched by any other major religious writing in history.

If the Bible revelation does not say you are God, or that you are chemicals without ultimate purpose, it certainly does not let you deal with plants as if *they* were just chemicals or interact with animals or living earth systems any way you want.

As a matter of fact, the sixth Commandment says, "You shall not murder" (Exodus 20:13, NIV). It does not say, "Do not murder *people,*" but, "Do not murder," which includes any selfish taking of life. So if you get violent one day and take out your anger on an innocent creation—including an animal, flower or tree, let alone another human being—you are in spirit violating that command.

The Bible teaches plainly that if we expect mercy we must be merciful, not only to our fellow humans but to all inferior animals. Every act of cruelty to animals, as well as to other human beings, is offensive to the Creator of all beings.

The lower animals look up to man for happiness just as man looks up to God. The Rev. Dr. Norman McLeod says, "I would not give much for the religion of any man or woman whose cat or dog were not the better for it."[10]

In light of what the Bible *actually* says about human responsibility under God for the land and the creation, who can claim that a Christian mandate on the environment is historic license to plunder, misuse and destroy God's creation? Whatever men and women have done with biblical commands, any such judgment, in light of Scripture's clear call to a profound healing of the land, can only be considered religious ignorance.

On the contrary, the Bible is the *one* major religious book in human history whose major metaphors are agricultural and conservationist. It is the only great book in history that provides a platform for real care of the creation, the only spiritual book that not only calls humanity to global responsibility, but gives a reason why humanity should even bother.

What the Bible Is Guilty Of

Three criticisms of the Bible message *are* true.

◄► First, this Book does portray mankind as set over the creation. Unashamedly it proclaims this to be so.

◄► It is also true that the Bible does not speak of all life as being intrinsically one with God. It takes pains to show that humanity is made different from the rest of the creation. The Bible, neither an Eastern nor a Western book, distinguishes between the various forms of animate creation and the God-breathed origin of mankind.

↝ Finally, although both mankind and nature are part of the creation, the Bible shows clearly that the creation is not part of its Creator. There is a distinction between God the Creator, an infinite Person, and the creation, which is finite.

The Unity of the Universe

Do you remember the hip Buddhist philosophy of the *Kung Fu* TV series in the late '60s and early '70s of being "one with the universe"? Many '90s thinkers have never gotten over the optimistic romance of that esoteric era. And in a great deal of New Age thought, the reason we should love the planet is Spinoza's idea that we are "one with the trees."

What happens in a very practical way when you believe that all life is one on that level? As Francis Schaeffer pointed out, you don't bring the grass up to the level of man; you bring humanity down to the level of the grass.

If your problem (as the story goes) is that you just don't realize you are one with God, then you feel pain, dislocation and loneliness only because you think somehow you are different, separate, unlike. Although you actually are God, you have somehow forgotten it. (Silly you! We won't ask *how* you came to forget that.) Your task, then (we are told), is simply to relearn it.

In a world of separation, fragmentatation and division, in which people long for a sense of closeness to one another, to their world and to nature, this old idea is attractive. And it contains something close enough to truth to capture the hearts and imaginations of millions of people. To really be *one* with everything! To eliminate the barriers, do away with divisions, remove the roadblocks. Isn't this the true answer to it all?

The sad fact is, no. Close but no cigar. The Eastern idea of unity attempted by millions—from the self-denying Hindu holy man to the channeling New Age homemaker—has a worm in its attractive apple.

The Worm in the Apple

If matter is evil or illusory, if the whole of the world around us is only a dream, then right and wrong have no corresponding basis in the material world.

And if at heart life is one grand illusion, then nothing other than final emancipation from the evil of matter—*by losing our own "false" identity*—can be the solution. Recall the message of *The Nectar of Devotion*: "Spirit soul in its original condition is joyful, blissful, eternal and full of knowledge. Only by implication in material activities has he become miserable, temporary and full of ignorance."

The real answer to the problems of our world, according to Eastern philosophy, is first to understand it as unreal, then to leave it forever. There is no escape other than annihilation of the self. Unity is achieved at the cost of your own identity.

Denial and death. There's no other way.

The Biblical Answer

What is the basis of real *unity* with God and nature? The link of humanity with God is certainly not on the level of some blending with the infinite, in either substance or knowledge. "Canst thou by searching," asked Job, "find out God?" (Job 11:7a). On a knowledge basis, the finite can never become one with the infinite.

Equally obviously, the creation (a "made") will never share the same substance as the uncreated ("unmade") Creator. We will never in some mystical way share a common consciousness of "being God" so that we will know one day that you, me, the flea, the sea and the redwood tree are all in final reality "one with Him." Put simply, God's stuff is wholly and forever unlike the stuff of everything else He made. Even He cannot make an unmade. No creation can or ever will become God.

Is there then no hope of unity with God? If we cannot evolve to His level of knowledge, or be like Him in substance, how can we ever know Him?

The Bible answer is profound. The link between God and humanity is that God Himself is a divine Person and made us also as persons. We as finite persons can never know Him exhaustively, nor become one with Him in substance, as the East attempts to do metaphysically. But we can know Him *morally*, for He is a Person and created us in His own moral image. And we can know Him genuinely through Jesus Christ, His Son.

This is the core message of the Gospel. This is why so many millions of people down through the centuries, and all over the world as part of the largest belief system on our planet, have gladly testified that real unity with God is not only possible in Jesus Christ, but a possessible reality.

And how do we link with nature? Although the Bible is careful to distinguish mankind from the rest of creation, we are all creatures. We share a common createdness. Thus we have common responsibility, each on our own level of sentience, awareness and capacity, to honor and acknowledge God as our Creator and celebrate our own place in His creation.

The Problem with Creation

To mankind has been given the honor and privilege of administering this creation as its appointed crowned representative under God. We have, as God's chosen representatives, been placed over this finite creation to "be fruitful, and multiply, and replenish the earth, and subdue it: and have dominion"—to reapportion or reallocate the resources where they properly belong.

If our ancestors had been faithful to heed this Genesis call, we would to this day have a wonderful world. But tragedy has happened. According to Scripture (as we saw in chapter 2), a fall in space and time has taken place that plunged our world into disarray. Neither man nor his environment nor animals nor plants now live the way they were designed. Surrounded by the consequences of this aberration and blinded by our modern materialistic mindset, we now read the structures of nature in ways that often prove utterly wrong.

Our problem with limited resources is not primarily over-population; it is greed. Our problem with pollution is not the invention of fluorocarbons or mass transport; it is irresponsibility. The loss of an acre of forest every second, the mass slaughter of elephants for their ivory, the extinction of entire species of plants, insects and animals all over the world is not something that "just happens" because there are more of us human beings. It happens because the race of ruling beings put in charge has almost wholly lost its sense of stewardship. We have turned away from God.

The answer is not just adopting any old religious view; *it is individual, national and global repentance.* And in that costly but centrally essential act lies the moral key to the ecological crisis.

In Part 2, let's look again—much closer up this time—at our poor, broken world, and how we can safely treat it as one great system needing divine and human care.

Part 2

A World
of Wonder

The more unintelligent a man is, the less mysterious existence seems to him.

Arthur Shopenhauer

An undevout astronomer is mad.

Edward Young

My cat and dog live together in my house and seem to like it. It may have been one of man's functions to restore peace to the animal world, and if he had not joined the enemy, he might have succeeded in doing so to an extent now hardly imaginable.

C. S. Lewis

5

Earth Is Unique

Speak to the earth, and it shall teach thee. . . .

Job 12:8

Praise ye him, sun and moon: praise him, all ye stars of light.

Psalm 148:3

Some think there are as many stars in the universe as there are grains of sand on all the seashores of earth. If so, our particular spot in this corner of the cosmos is very, very special.

Life on Earth

In the early 1960s, astronomers like Carl Sagan and the Russian Iosef Shklovsky said that perhaps as many as 0.001% of the stars (one in every thousand) could have planets that might support earth-type life. This was an educated guess, of course. You cannot actually see any planets around even the closest stars; they are just too far away.

But that estimate also turns out to be far too optimistic. We are still looking today for one star with planets that might support earth-type life. There might be a planet around Barnard's Star and possibly a few more elsewhere. (These are calculated by observing tiny differences in the way light reaches us.) But pickings are slim. Evidence is hard to come by.

There is even the astonishing possibility that, apart from a few local exceptions, there are no other planets beyond our own solar system!

What has happened since the 1960s? Since those early optimistic estimates, we have had time for a good, hard look at the facts about our universe, and in particular our planet. We have sent out deep-space probes, manned Moon-landers and unmanned Mars-landers. Most have reported back faithfully and told us what many scientists and science fiction writers did not actually want to know: that when it comes to finding planets like ours, the possibility is less and less likely all the time.

We know much more now than we did in the '60s. Our previous estimates for the number of possible life-supporting planets must now feed through a growing number of excluding parameters, possibility screens or grids determined by physical laws that narrow down the chance much more.

Criteria Essential for Life

In his book *The Fingerprint of God*, the Christian astronomer Hugh Ross outlines some of the more than forty different criteria essential for life to exist. These "life filters" determine whether life is possible on a planet.

Dr. Ross is a Christian voice among at least nine other scientists who, like him, are deeply moved by these discoveries. The critical balancing factors in recent studies by scientists like Paul Davies (*God, Physics and the New Astronomy*) and George Greenstein (*The Symbiotic Universe*) point irresistibly to an astonishing conclusion called **the anthropic principle**: Life on earth, an exquisite harmony of critical factors, seems peculiarly designed for humans being and other living things. So many things are just right for life, in fact, that all the old guesses of "happening by chance" go right out the window.

Not only does earth, from the data, seem designed specifically for humans, but *seemingly designed by a Person*. As Greenstein writes:

> As we survey all the evidence, the thought consistently arises that some supernatural agency (or rather Agency) must be involved. Is it possible that suddenly and without intending to, we have stumbled upon the scientific proof of the existence of the Supreme Being? Was it God Who stepped in and so providentially crafted the cosmos for our benefit?[1]

Although most of these scientists are not professed believers, they are compelled by the sheer weight of evidence to acknowledge that earth is utterly unique, and that in its specialness our planet is apparently "anthropic"—designed for mankind.

Unlike anyplace else in our universe, which consists of at least a hundred billion trillion stars, earth sits as the crown jewel. The rest of creation seems to serve simply as a setting and service for this one planet that the Bible says God visited with life.

Let's take a closer look at why it seems increasingly certain that, so far as earth is concerned, there really is "no place like home."

The Stuff of the Universe

"A Cosmic Collector's Piece"

We now know that only a few stars (of the right age and type) in only a few places can form life-supporting planets. You will not find them near the center of a galaxy or near the edges of it, but about two-thirds from the center. This is where our sun "happens" to be.

Only forty percent of the stars are the right color (meaning the right temperature and spectrum for photosynthesis) and only a few (two in ten thousand) are the right size.

As far as the stuff of the rest of our universe is concerned, our sun is pretty normal, while earth, and the kind of materials that make it up as a planet, is a rare speck in a universe made up largely of gases like hydrogen and helium—the simplest and most abundant two elements around. We are, said Fred Hoyle, a "cosmic collector's piece." So as far as most of the rest of the universe is concerned, earth is made of the "wrong stuff."

We find fully 92% of the elements of the known universe to be *hydrogen*, the explosive gas used in dirigibles until the Hindenburg disaster. Nearly eight percent of the elements remaining is *helium*, the gas they use to blow up your kid's balloon or make your voice squeaky. Only a tiny fraction of the rest of the universe (0.001%) contains heavier elements, like the ones that make up the rocks and surface of our planet. (To get those elements, astronomers believe that a planet has to draw from the ash of old stars that form these elements and be near enough to supernovas that make up the other needed elements for life.)

Of these "trace" constituents, observes Carl Sagan in his paper on "The Primordial UV Synthesis of Nucleoside Phosphates," "Only carbon, nitrogen and oxygen are both reactive and relatively abundant." And *carbon*, the "Lego of life" (the foundation element of living things on this planet), is still extremely rare in the universe, as are heavier crust elements like iron, aluminum, silicon and other substances that make a technical civilization like ours possible.

Even the *oxygen* so abundant in water all over our planet, making life possible to us who breathe it in our atmosphere, is little more than a trace element in the universe.

What do you suppose the odds are that many other planets exist with these same tiny trace elements, as ours does, making it possible for life to exist and for complex civilizations to be built?

Other elements can form complex chains, of course—elements like *silicon* (the basic material of sand) for transistors and integrated circuits that make modern electronics possible. But silicon does not react nearly so easily or so well with other elements like carbon, and many of its reactions require exotic reagents and/or very high temperatures.

Without the ability to form complex chains, the chemical frame within which high-order design or intelligence can be stored cannot exist. Put simply, *If it cannot be complex, it cannot be used to store much sense.* Silicon-based life forms are possible, but not on a planet like ours, and not on any planet you would like to live on.

"It's Life, Jim, but Not as We Know It"

The odds that life on earth arose by accident are astronomical enough. The odds of similar life arising the same way somewhere else in the universe are dim indeed. Do any stars have planets like earth? The more you learn, the less likely it seems.

Let's look at some of the factors critical for a living planet.

The Type of Star

A planet without a star would be too cold to support life. If it had more than one star, huge gravitic interactions would disrupt its very orbit.

⇥ Then again, a planet has to have the right kind of star. Neither new nor old stars burn stably; our sun is right in the middle of a star's life cycle with its finest years ahead.

⇥ The *size* of the star is critical; it cannot be too big or too small, and only two stars in every ten thousand, as I said before, fill the bill.

⇥ If our own sun were *bigger*, it would burn too radically and quickly. Smaller stars are stable. But if ours were *smaller*, it would have to be closer for earth to have a water cycle. The temperature then might be right, but even a small shift of our planet closer to the sun would trigger terrible tidal destruction.

63

The Size of the Planet

The size of the planet plays a crucial role in determining what kind of gases make up its atmosphere. A planet's mass determines its "escape velocity," the speed and mass a body needs to pull away from its gravitational field. Gases are trapped or lost depending on their weight, and earth has just the right mix of gases to sustain a high order of life.

If our planet were *bigger,* like Jupiter, the atmosphere would never lose poisonous gases like methane and ammonia. (A deep sniff of your well-diluted "window-cleaner with ammonia" bottle will give you an idea of what that "fresh air" might smell like!) Venus is terribly hot with an atmosphere of concentrated sulphuric acid.

If earth were *smaller,* on the other hand, like Mercury, it would lose too much water vapor. Our planet would rapidly become an arid, plant-less desert and die.

Apart from poisonous gases, there are other ramifications of size. What if earth *were* much bigger? There would be more room, all right. But then you would have to weigh a hundred or maybe even a thousand times more than you do now, when looking at the scale is embarrassing enough as it is! And if you wanted to move, you couldn't.

Why not? Because the physical frames of living things have a structure, and there is a practical limit to the weight of that structure. Weight is determined by the gravity of a planet, which is determined in turn by its size and density. The heaviest and tallest men in history all had the same problem: The more they grew, the less they could move, so that near the end of their lives they were almost unable to walk. Flesh can sustain only so much of a load (as all the Weight Watchers and Jenny Craig customers know).

If earth were much larger and we were hundreds of times heavier, our carbon-based tissue strength could not handle our free-standing loads. In short, our own weight would crush us. (So much for the science fiction movies on giant spiders and ants! Forget it. They couldn't move. Their mutant size would crush their innards.)

Also, have you noticed how often little kids trip and rarely seem to break anything? Adults trip and break bones readily. A six-foot adult who falls has two hundred times the force of child tripping. So if we were much bigger, we would smash ourselves up over everything; and if earth were very much bigger, you would resemble a dumpling. A dead one.

The Distance of the Planet from Its Sun

We are just right in distance (93 million miles) from a sun that is just the right size (a million miles in diameter), and we travel around it at just the right-shaped orbit (nearly circular).

⤙ Get a planet *too close* to a sun and everything on it boils away like Death Valley on a record high. Put it *farther away* and the planet becomes too cold, an ice planet worse than Hoth of the second Star Wars sequel. Distance is critical. Half a million miles either way—a mere one percent change in the vast distances of space—and life on earth would cease to exist.

⤙ We have already seen that without the ability to form complex chains, the chemical frame within which high-order design or intelligence can be stored cannot exist. Because carbon has the ability to form complex chains with other key elements, and because carbon is one of the few chemicals with possibilities complex enough to hold high-order information, carbon chains form the basis of many of the basic building blocks of which we are made.

⤙ But these chains form only within a *fairly narrow temperature range*. The chemical complexity of a brain of even a thick-witted person can form only within the chemical reaction range of temperatures that happens to be available on earth, facilitated by the distance from the earth to the sun.

The Rate of Revolution

The rate of revolution of a planet—how fast it turns—determines, among other things, the form of its atmosphere. The particular form of air we breathe is possible because every day and night the plants work to give us renewed skies.

We breathe out carbon dioxide all the time; it is one key waste product of the way we get energy from food. And, wonderfully enough, plants love and live off of what we leave! Plants take in this same CO_2, along with some minerals from the soil and water. They use the energy of light from the particular wavelengths of our sun, turn this waste into their own growth as food energy and give back to us in the air the oxygen we need to live.

A kilogram (2.2 lbs.) of a sun-loving healthy plant like spinach stores enough chlorophyll in its wet leaves to make a couple of liters of oxygen every hour out of the carbon dioxide in our air (0.03–0.04%). Even algae, that lowly, green, slimy stuff around ponds, is awesome at photosynthesis. If the carbon dioxide in our air jumped up to as high as one percent, algae is capable, provided it gets the light it needs, of more than doubling its conversion rate to oxygen.

And every new day the earth turns, the plants get busy and the air is renewed. If there were no such cycle, the plants could not turn carbon dioxide back into oxygen and we would all start to die.

If you were a plant, your favorite soap opera would be *As the World Turns.* Earth spins, not only giving us a normalized temperature, but giving the plants dark and light cycles for much-needed rest.

What if our days were longer? All the plants would burn or freeze. If earth took any longer to turn—say, thirty hours instead of 24—our days would be too hot and nights too cold to sustain life. *If earth turned any faster* (like Jupiter, which whips around in just ten hours), you would see winds, storms and tornadoes like you wouldn't believe. Even on a quiet day, winds on Jupiter reach 1,000 miles an hour!

Earth, Wind and Fire

The Air

Not only these initial factors are crucial for life. Also crucial is the way elements must stay mixed, proportioned and balanced. We take for granted a simple act like lighting a fire. Yet the percentage of oxygen to nitrogen and carbon dioxide in the air needed for a fire is critical.

٭ We have about 21% of oxygen in proportion to the other gases so that everything burns nicely. With just a little *more oxygen* in the atmosphere, plants and other hydrocarbons would burn too easily. If the proportion went up four percent and you lit a fire, everything carbon-based on earth might catch fire, too, and everything would begin to burn!

٭ Billy Joel sang "We Didn't Start the Fire," but one thing is certain: If the air we breathe were a little bit richer in oxygen, we could never stop any fire once it started. Yet if we had fifteen percent *less oxygen*, we could never get anything to burn, and much of our civilization would not be possible. With less oxygen we would find it hard to breathe, like a person with a continual asthma attack. As nothing would burn, combustion would be impossible: No campfires, no cooking, certainly no cars!

٭ We have all heard of the *ozone barrier* in our upper atmosphere. If it were much *thinner,* ultraviolet radiation from the sun would become ultra-violent to living tissues like skin (hence the current concern over skin cancer), and the surface temperature of the land would become unbearable. If the ozone layer were much *thicker,* the land would not receive enough heat.

٭ If the *ratio of light reflected* back into space from the surface of the earth (its "albedo") were either too much or too little, we would have either a runaway ice age or an accelerating "greenhouse" heating effect. As it is, the ratio of reflected light is just right.

The Earth

The proportion of land to water on earth is unique in the solar system, and quite probably the universe. The proportion is just right for "irrigation." Earth's stunning blue-green appearance from space indicates its utterly special design; we live on a water-abundant planet filled with vegetation that needs moist air to irrigate land.

◄► One of the strange things about earth is its *tilt* as it turns. This steady, small, off-center angle—caused and made steady, as we now know, by the gravitational influence of the moon—gives us our seasons around the world. You may go somewhere sunny during the winter or head for the snows on another part of the planet when it gets too hot, but have you ever thought what happens to mosquitoes and other bugs in the winter? Especially bacteria, the sort that multiply in warm, muggy climates.

Imagine what would happen to people's health if it was hot and humid all the time! The earth's tilt causing some seasonal variation (unless you live in a country like Singapore) is one of the factors that spare us from epidemical destruction.

What would earth be like without its tilt? Not only would we not have seasons, but losing this moderating balance would allow disease-carrying bacteria to multiply alarmingly. We might soon see accelerating outbreaks of all kinds of sickness, not only in human beings but in bird and animal life—the disabling or death of most of the world.

◄► The *earth's crust* is sometimes shaken by earthquakes and volcanoes; but if it were much *thicker*, too much oxygen would be pulled into it out of our atmosphere. If it were much *thinner*, we would live on a movie set of *Earthquake* or *The Last Days of Pompeii*. If we had substantially *more earthquakes,* life as we know it would end; but if we had substantially *fewer,* nutrients on the ocean floors from river runoffs would not recycle back to the continents and the land would get progressively poorer. Even dangerous geological events are sometimes part of the checks and balances that make life possible.

Mysteries of the Universe

Size

The sheer size of the universe has been one of the most mind-boggling discoveries of human history. And it certainly is big. Hugh Ross illustrates the enormous distances between the stars with a baseball. If our sun (a million miles in diameter) were the size of a baseball in southern California, the next star to ours would be in Peru or Siberia. Then imagine more than a hundred billion trillion of the stars in the known universe similarly spread out. The creation is indeed mind-boggling in its size and scope.

This size is a testimony to something even more marvelous. If all the glorious cosmos were brought into being instantly at the command of God, you begin to touch the edge of just how great the creative majesty is that built the worlds. With God, the creation of the whole of the wheeling universe is "all in a day's work."

When you further think that everything is up there only for background decoration until the coming main event, the recreation of new heavens and a new earth for the housing of God's ultimate creation project, you get an inkling of the staggering greatness and majesty of God.

It is certainly possible that the universe could have been smaller. But there are some nice things about its being so big. It is humbling to discover just how small we are in relation to everything around us. David said it best: "When I consider thy heavens, the work of thy fingers, the moon and the stars, which thou hast ordained; what is man, that thou art mindful of him? . . ." (Psalm 8:3–4).

You would probably like my business card. One of my friends and I were talking about what it means to belong to Christ and be part of His purposes, and how difficult it is to convey how wonderful this "forever family" is. When people ask me what I do, I don't want a card that might cause misconceptions. If I put a cross on my card, they might think I manage a mausoleum or funeral parlor. If I put a fish on it, they might think I own a pet shop.

Larry and I came up with something different. My visiting card is a metallic silver spiral nebula on a black-on-black background. It says *Galactic Management Associates* in large letters along the top, and in smaller print along the bottom, *Family Owned and Operated.*

Now when people ask me what I do for a living, I tell them, "I'm in a management training program." And when they ask what I am training for, I tell them offhandedly, "Oh, I'm just in training to help rule and reign over the universe."

Oddly enough, I am absolutely serious.

How Quick a Creation?

The sheer size of our universe raises another question. People often ask, "How is it conceivable for any complex creation, let alone one of this magnitude, to come about so fast? Didn't all this demand long amounts of time?"

Bible scholars and believing scientists have thought about this for a long time, and of course there are sincerely different Christian responses. Some, like Hugh Ross, think that the days mentioned in Genesis might have been eons—long ages, possibly. In this theory, the "days" of earth's creation might in "real" time have taken millions of years. Others think that physical constants like light velocity might initially have been different, so that time itself might have changed.

Yet strangely enough, the simple statement of the Genesis record that all this vast wonder was created in a short time can still make sense. An event of near-instantaneous creation cannot be ruled out simply because we cannot conceive of something so vast and complex being formed so quickly.

Henry Ford built a car and it took him eighteen years. Ford Motor Company builds cars now and I imagine you can see one completed (with some incentive!) in less than eighteen hours. That would be exceptional but it is certainly not a miracle. If you bring in a dedicated team and large bonuses, it is not inconceivable at some point that a car could be assembled in eighteen minutes. (A street gang can certainly strip one faster than that!)

Creation time is simply a function of *collected energy, resources and intelligence.* How you shrink eighteen years to eighteen hours or even, with future technology, to eighteen minutes is determined by available energy (in this case, machines amplifying the work of people's hands), resources assembled and ready at hand, and the intelligence of more than a century of knowledge in car-making stored in the computer chips that drive the metal-fabricating machines. The greater the energy, available resources and intelligence, the faster the possible creation time. It is, as Mr. Spock of the old Starship Enterprise would say, "entirely logical."

Theoretically, then, there is no problem with the concept of a short creation time. It all depends on how much power, resources and wisdom are available to the Creator. *Given God, even a young universe is possible!*

The current consensus among most scientists, of course, is that our universe must be old. We have no way of visualizing anything else, especially if all of life here arose by accident. Yet despite this consensus, some discoveries seem to indicate that earth and even the universe are younger than they seem. Some odd things we have found out recently—the thinness of moon dust, for example, and the existence of pleochroic haloes in rocks—seem to indicate not only a designed universe, but a relatively recent creation, a young earth.

People themselves appear to be relatively recent. Scientists have discovered things like apparent human footprints, a human fossil finger and a human fossil tooth in the same strata as authenticated dinosaur tracks—even a fossil human skull discovered in a coal bed!

So I have neither a philosophical nor a theological problem with a quick or even instantaneous creation. How fast can you make something if you have infinite power, wisdom and unlimited resources? No, my problem is different: Given the fact that this awesome and wonderful God did create our original world, *why did He take so long?*

Part of the answer may be: *For our sakes.* Doing things just before the arrival of special guests tends to suggest (however inaccurate the perception) a lack of preparation, forethought, expectation. So it is possible that God wanted us to know we were prepared for. This astonishing universe was built to focus on this planet, on *you* as the crown of all God's creation. You are not simply an accidental byproduct. You are loved.

God's Design Humor

Our own solar system has all kinds of new puzzles in it. When we sent *Explorer* on a fly-by past Saturn, for instance, we found that some of the mysterious rings of this planet are intertwined, actually sort of braided.

But how Saturn's rings could be like this is a real mystery. If they have been there for millions of years, they would not, by all the laws of physics, be like that; they would have achieved unity. So either the rings are relatively recent, or else Saturn itself is relatively recent.

In any case, God has done unusual things. I think He did much of creation just for fun, while His sense of design humor gives materialists and skeptics some sleepless nights.

Venus and Uranus not only rotate in the *opposite* direction from all the other planets in our solar system, but about *one-third* of the moons in our planetary system go "backwards." Quirks like this drive scientists crazy who think we all condensed out of a Swedenborgian vision of a rotating gas and dust cloud. It is hard to think of some "accident" big enough to wholly reverse a moon's orbit without shattering it, let alone the spin direction of a whole planet.

Perhaps exceptions to the general rule like this are God's gentle, silent way of saying, "Now, do I have your attention?"

One in a Cosmic Trillion

These, then, are just a few of the critical factors that show earth as utterly unique and that, in exquisite harmony, make life on earth appear peculiarly designed for mankind. Dr. Ross and his staff estimate that the chance of a place like earth happening accidentally—even using only thirty of the more than forty significant global and galactic factors that govern possible life—are only *one in a hundred billion trillion trillion*. Even if every star in every galaxy had a planetary system, the chance of a place like earth coming into being, with its teeming harmony of life, is one in a cosmic trillion.

And only a Person, in this scientist's view, could have engineered someplace as perfect for living things as earth.[2]

6

Three Life
Exceptions
to Natural Law

Nature, to be commanded, must be obeyed.

Francis Bacon

What, then, is Nature, and how do we come to be impris-
oned in a system so alien to us? Oddly enough, the question
becomes much less sinister the moment one realizes that
Nature is not all. Mistaken for our mother, she is terrifying
and even abominable. But if she is only our sister—if she and
we have a common Creator—if she is our sparring partner—
then the situation is quite tolerable.

C. S. Lewis

The more we look at the uniqueness of life, the more astonishing it appears. We saw in the last chapter, on a galactic and
planetary scale, how many critical life factors must be harmo-
nized in delicate balance for organic survival. Despite the fact
that since the turn of the century we have moved away from even
the idea of cause and effect in our quantum-mechanics interpretation of the nature of deep reality, in actual practice life has

rules. In light of the rules of physics, the fact that we exist at all is a miracle. Yet in our gaze up and out through the mysterious universe, we must not miss the wonders right under our nose.

In this chapter I would like to consider three extraordinary exceptions to laws that govern the basics of our very existence—laws that deal respectively with *water, air* and *sunlight.* When we look from a certain critical level at the usual behavior of liquids, gases and hot substances, three natural laws seem to be broken. *If this were not true, moreover, life would not be possible here on earth.*

What Laws Mean—and Don't Mean

But first understand this: No law in the universe ever *caused* anything. A law only describes how things react and interrelate, how material reality operates. Life has rules; to try to break them may mean death. But to think that law causes anything is like thinking, "Because I can count, I'm rich." Laws simply show us how things work.

To a Christian, moreover, laws are not autonomous; they do not exist independent of the sustaining hand of God. God has covenanted to act faithfully, and we can count on Him to act consistently in all levels of reality.

The law we call "gravity" is one such description. Technically it has to do with the "inverse square of the distance between the centers of two masses." But imagine on a practical level what would happen if gravity shifted capriciously from day to day.

Life would be weird. You would have to wear magnetic boots and seatbelts on every chair. Cars would have to dig their way in as we drove them, in order to stay down. If gravity were arbitrary and you happened to hit the wrong cycle, you would accelerate one moment at 32 feet per second up and away from earth, only to fall back at precisely the same speed a few seconds later!

No scientist ever sat down and said, "Hmm, I think I'll create something called gravity." Rather, the law of gravity—and all natural law—is the testimony of creation to the faithfulness of God. The fact that these laws are stable is wonderful. The key word when we think about the harmony of relationships in our physical universe is *faithful.*

It is important to see that God still deals actively with humanity and nature. He is involved intimately with His creation. We do not have a universe once wound up like a watch and then walked out on. This Deistic picture of God as absent Clockmaker has been popular from time to time. Sometimes even Christians forget God is neither asleep nor absent, let alone dead or gone.

Yet even in law God reserves the right to intervene. God is not only faithful but capable of miracle. His special intervention is not really the "breaking" of law, but the application of a higher law in special circumstances. If we believe with the deists of previous centuries that God wound up the universe and walked out, or with the materialists of this century that life and all its laws here are a closed system, we will not allow any sort of miracle. In fact, we will often be blind to any sort of special exemption to the rule, and refuse to acknowledge anything as true that does not fit into the general pattern.

But if we do so, we will be wrong. Even in physics there are exceptions to usually consistent patterns.

In the next three subsections I want to amplify what Arthur Custance observed originally in his wonderful *Doorway Paper* studies on science and faith[1]—three exceptions to the norm that happen in life, laws that seem to be "broken" in our world. Fundamentals govern nature, and while no actual law is broken in the examples we examine here, in three special circumstances the usual is excepted. If it were not, none of us would be alive.

Water: A Chemical Parable

The first of these anomalies in nature involves liquids. When a liquid gets colder it gets denser; as it cools, it becomes more tightly packed. This is true with any and all liquids except one—

water. Before seeing how this works, let's review a few important facts about water.

Endangered

Water is the most common chemical compound on earth. It is so abundant that if all land were level, it would cover our planet uniformly to a depth of one and a half miles.

But although it is the most common element on our planet, it is on the endangered list. "Safe drinking water for all by the year 1990": This proposal was made by the World Health Organization in 1980 and seemed within reach at the time. Yet in 1990 some 2.2 billion people (42% of the world) still had no adequate water supply.[2] And only a tiny portion of water is available for drinking.

> Only 3% of the earth's water is fresh and almost 90% of that is trapped in glaciers or in the atmosphere or absorbed by the ground. In fact, if all the water in the world were reduced to one gallon, the portion of it that would be both fresh and available for human consumption would be less than two hundredths of a teaspoon. Not enough to make a decent drip.[3]

Mysterious

Although it is the best-known and most-studied compound on earth, ordinary water remains a mystery. We know that its chemical formula is H_2O, but we do not know fully how it behaves with the millions of compounds that react in it. (More substances dissolve in water than in any other liquid.)

A water molecule has an unusual structure, like a mini-magnet, with a positive charge on one side and a negative charge on the other, so that one side or the other can attach itself to another molecule, whatever its charge. And water is the only compound whose chemical bonds react at a low enough energy level not to tear apart the life design molecules that depend on it for exchange and combination.

Even absolutely "pure" water is composed of at least 33 substances, made up of various combinations of the three isotopes of hydrogen and oxygen and different sorts of water ions created by out-of-place electrons. To top off all this wonder, a lake of water may really be only *one laced great molecule.* All the oceans on earth, then, could be approximated scientifically as $H_2 \times 10^{46}O \times 10^{46}$!

Although the hydrogen-oxygen bonds in water are only about ten percent as strong as most other chemical bonds, they stick to one another tenaciously and require enormous energy to pull them apart. Extremely pure water has the pulling power of a strong cable that can pull its own weight easily as high as nine thousand feet—almost two miles. Most other simple compounds containing hydrogen boil away more easily. (Methane, for instance, is liquid only at $-161°$ Centigrade.)

The First Extraordinary Exception

These special bonds explain why it takes great energy to change ice to water and water to steam, which is why water heats up so slowly. Water is also unique in that it occurs naturally in all three normal states of matter: solid (ice), liquid (water) and gas (water vapor, as in clouds and steam).

At a particular point as water is cooled—near 39° Fahrenheit and 4° Centigrade—water (which has been obeying the norm and getting denser up to that point) stops and actually gets "looser." By natural law it ought not to do that, but it does!

How does this happen? The secret lies in its very structure. When the water molecules link to form the pattern of an ice crystal, their unique shape creates a gap between them, *increasing* the amount of space they take up.

What does this mean in practical terms in nature? It means that when the top layer of water on a pond gets cold and freezes, because the slightly warmer water underneath it is denser, the newly formed ice will not sink. This is vital because the ice then floats; it is actually "lighter" than cold water. Now you can cut it out as blocks for your igloo, float it on top of your drink, even skate on it if it is thick enough.

Why is this significant? Because this ice (the most perfectly bonded hydrogen structure known) now forms an *insulating layer* and helps keep the rest of the river water from getting too cold. All the aquatic plant life and pond fish are covered in *from the top down*, not frozen out from the bottom up.

So that odd property of water, making it unlike all other substances, "just happens" to ensure life on this planet. Fortunate coincidence?

Water is unique in being most dense these few degrees above its melting point. No other liquid behaves like this. Yet how casually we treat this incredibly designed substance!—so rare in the rest of the universe, so wonderfully engineered for sustaining life on all levels on our planet.

Water is a chemical parable. Without this "simple" substance, all life on earth would perish. No wonder Jesus said, "I am the water of life." Water is the single-most important substance for life on earth.

Air: When Lighter Is Heavier

What about our air? Gases, like other substances, are (as you would imagine) obliged to behave according to the law of gravity. Here is one obvious way of saying it: What goes up must come down. Heavy things move to the bottom, light things move to the top. Simple. Soap is somewhere on the bottom of your bathwater; the bubbles are on top.

But if the principle that heavy stuff sinks to the bottom and light stuff rises to the top were always true among the gases, as for everything else, we would be in serious trouble with our atmosphere (more than we are now). In fact, we would all be dead.

The Second Extraordinary Exception

We have already observed that we breathe out carbon dioxide as the waste byproduct of our own respiration cycle. Carbon dioxide is also the better part of the waste products of cars burning petroleum. It cannot support breathing or burning. We cannot live in carbon dioxide.

But here is the paradox. Carbon dioxide is heavier than oxygen, so by rights it should fall to the bottom layer of gases in our atmosphere, the layer available to us near the ground, while oxygen, which is lighter (not to mention breathable), should be forced above the layer of carbon dioxide, where we could not get to it.

You would expect there to be, according to the law of gravity, a thickening killer blanket of carbon dioxide from the ground up covering the earth. (We are currently working on this killer blanket with more dangerous emissions from cars and factories.) But here is the second exception. The law of gravity is "defied" by another law, *the diffusion of gases*. Because of this law that seemingly overrides the law of gravity, the heavier carbon dioxide actually migrates up through the atmosphere, while lighter oxygen forms a blanket beneath it. Carbon dioxide diffuses through the other gases of the atmosphere, making oxygen available to breathe.

That is a second seeming violation of natural law and a reason we are all still alive. Another anomaly, "a deep thought." Think about it.

Sunlight: Free to Keep Shining

Finally, consider the gift of sunlight. Our sun, a "G1"-type pulsing dwarf star, yellow in color, contains at least 63 known elements and eleven molecules. The greatest percentage of its makeup, like most of the rest of the matter in the universe (as I already mentioned), is hydrogen being converted slowly to helium (15%). So though the sun is much larger than our earth, it is not as dense.

Temperatures on the Sun

Temperatures even on the surface of the sun (which is one of the "cooler" stars in the universe) are still mind-boggling: We measure them at about 10,800 degrees Fahrenheit (almost 6,000 degrees Centigrade)!

Some of the other "cooler" (redder) stars in space seem to contain even higher proportions of heavier trace elements like carbon, beryllium, boron and oxygen. Scientists think these elements are formed as byproducts of thermonuclear reactions. Suns are basically big fusion reactors. Energy flows from them in the form of light and heat created as byproducts when the nuclei of an element like hydrogen combine to form a heavier element like helium. Then its radiated energy is not like that of a big coal furnace but from the actual transformation of small amounts of matter to energy in an atomic process—a fusion reaction.

The Law

If you studied chemistry in school, did you ever heat something to help a reaction start? If you looked at the mixture and nothing seemed to be happening, you stuck it into a test tube and held it over a Bunsen burner. Then things probably got going.

The reason: At higher temperatures chemical reactions speed up, and at lower temperatures chemical reactions slow down. If you lower the temperature too much, combustion is impossible. You cannot burn something too cold. But as the temperature rises, combustion becomes more and more possible, until finally you can get oxides even from metals and other harder substances—because at high temperatures things burn better.

So here is the law: The higher the temperature, the more energy is released into chemical bonds, and the greater the possibility for combinations. The higher the temperature, the greater the complexity and the more things a substance will combine with.

That's nice, isn't it? This law makes it possible for us to form all kinds of new and complex compounds—simply by taking them to higher temperatures. Higher temperatures allow greater combinations in nature.

Until the temperatures get *very* high. Then you get our third exception.

The Third Extraordinary Exception

At solar temperatures the rules change. Chemical reactions actually reverse themselves.

We would expect something as hot as the sun to form a lot of material. But (and here is the paradox) if that actually happened with a star like the sun, its products of combustion would create a "solar ash" and it would quickly choke itself out.

So another "exception" to the rules keeps us alive. At extremely high temperatures, like those of the sun, the normal rule does not apply. There, everything is reversed. Matter becomes not more complex but more simple. Even the elements lose their basic structure. Only a relatively small amount of combination is possible. Compounds disassociate. Things break down and are reduced to elemental states. Oxides are not formed.

If it were not for this odd fact of temperature reversal, our sun would go out.

So the sun keeps on giving light. And our planet, at least for the foreseeable future, stays warm and alive. A good thing, too! If we were to lose the heat of the sun, as we saw in the last chapter, everything within a short period would begin to die. Plants, no longer able to photosynthesize from sunlight, would stop making oxygen. And the air would soon become unbreathable.

You can imagine what a fright the religious scoffers around the cross got on the day Christ died. They said, "If You are really the Son of God, prove it." Then suddenly God switched out the light on earth for three hours (Matthew 27:45; Luke 23:44–45). Add to that the supernatural tearing of the veil in the Temple from top to bottom, a massive, rock-splitting earthquake and a multitude of close encounters with people walking around who were already dead and buried, and you have one really bad day for the professional skeptic. No wonder the record says that people were terrified (Matthew 27:54; Luke 23:48)!

Three laws. Three essential parameters for life on our world. Yet three curious "exceptions" allowing life actually to continue— a suspension of the normal rules by an odd, almost unnoticed twist to let life go on. These and other "curious exceptions" are the little oddities built into all existence.

We do not have to accept the biblical premise of personal design and providential order. We can adopt instead the notion that if a tree falls in the forest and nobody hears it fall, it makes no sound; that no order exists outside that imposed by our own minds; and that these life exceptions are merely mental constructions in a universe of chaos. But you will still have to seek regularity in the world around you in order to make sense of it and try to reorder it. And the further you get from God, the less you will understand His creation.

I want you to step out of our inherited Western rationalist assumptions and think *design*, think *purpose*; not "chemicals bumping into each other," but (built into the very structure of nature) a cooperative balance with odd design exceptions that demonstrate a wonderful providential care. God goes even further than these; He can (and sometimes does) actively reorder a pattern or structure.

God's "Gaps" in Natural Law

Many interesting accounts in the Bible illustrate God suspending or transcending the normal operation of things.

In the record of the young prophet who disobeyed God (1 Kings 13), the lion kills the prophet and never touches the donkey he is fleeing on. Yet to a lion, a donkey is like a T-bone steak. When the old prophet comes up, he sees the young prophet dead, the lion standing there and the donkey standing there, too—freaked out, maybe, but not trying to run away. An odd scenario, and a violation of normal and expected behavior in nature.

God reserves the right to intervene in His universe. Sometimes He does it in the *physical* world, sometimes in the *animate, non-moral* world, and sometimes even, as Pharaoh and Nebuchadnezzar found out, in the *moral* world (Proverbs 21:1). All the rules of created reality are subject to God's intervention, and sometimes His temporary override.

A professor of engineering in New Zealand gave me a copy of a book about God he had been working on. It was his vision of what he thought God must be like. One of his most interesting conclusions was this: Based on what he knew of nature, forgiveness is impossible.

This is what you would conclude, of course, looking at the laws of nature. They describe reality. They are impartial and inflexible. They do not allow exceptions. They do not "forgive" attempts to violate them. Rules show no mercy.

But the Bible reveals a wonderful truth: Even greater than the rules is the Ruler. And though He does not change the rules, nor make exceptions to the rules out of favoritism or sentimentality, He Himself can and does intervene on our behalf.

Mercy and Miracle

Nature shows God's justice and utter faithfulness. The engineering professor knew that. Nature is neither nice nor nasty; it is simply true to its laws.

But there is one truth the rules of nature cannot show us. The great Engineer Himself knows the design intimately, at all visible and invisible levels, and is capable of profoundly affecting each and any part of the system. The Ruler is also the Commander of nature. Miracles are not violations of law but "system access" by the Designer.

God is greater than His creation. He can step into the gap between cause and effect and even take a necessary consequence on Himself. In the cross of Christ, love transcended law. *At the heart of the universe is not mere justice but mercy.*

God speaks to a great fish and says, "Swallow that runaway rebellious preacher." The fish never says, "God, You know I can't stomach preachers." He just does it (Jonah 1:17).

The ravens feed God's prophet Elijah who, faithful to divine verdict, has called down an ecological nightmare on the land because of its sin. Those ravens bring him steak sandwiches every day, despite the fact that normally ravens would not only stay away from people but eat that lunch themselves (1 Kings 17:6).

85

The milk cows leave their crying calves shut up in the Philistine stalls and carry the Ark of God away instead, though they miss their babies terribly and moo all the way down the road to Jerusalem. Even a dumb Philistine with a bad case of divine hemorrhoids knows that something is going on that cannot be explained in the ordinary (1 Samuel 6).

But exceptions in nature are evidence that miracles and mercy are possible. *And if ever we needed mercy and miracle, it is now.*

7

Nature,
Soft of Foot and Fur

All things bright and beautiful,
All creatures great and small
And all things wise and wonderful;
The Lord God made them all.

Cecil F. Alexander

That was not first which is spiritual, but that which is natural; and afterward that which is spiritual.

1 Corinthians 15:46

If you are privileged to work with a good technical system, you do not need the designer looking constantly over your shoulder and asking, "Is it still working O.K.?" When an engineering team designs a complex system, they build in backups. Then, when something goes wrong along the way, the backups drop in to correct or compensate.

God forestructured life as an incredibly harmonious system—self-replicating, self-repairing and, to the most wonderful degree, self-correcting.

Henry Drummond said of creation:

> We fail to praise the ceaseless ministry of the great inanimate world around us only because its kindness is unobtrusive. Nature is always noiseless. . . . And we forget how truly every good and perfect gift comes from without and above because no pause in her changeless benefice teaches us the sad lessons of deprivation.[1]

The ordinary mechanisms of life, contrary to popular misconception, do not demand divine "intervention" to operate. To some extent they run independently. Life seems to run on its own. We do not see and may not know that the upholding of individual structured reality is by God's creative power. The structure itself is not usually recognized as the design evidence it really is. People mistake a self-running, self-correcting system for one that arrived at order somehow on its own.

Yet this automation of life is its own silent witness; it has been put into place with such genius that it needs no supervision. It is the ultimate expert system, the highest example of marvelous design. Only when one of its operating subsystems begins to break down (sickness) or is ultimately threatened (impending death) do people think of calling on the Designer at all.

Key differences exist between humankind and the rest of the lower creation. Animals, for example, do not seem to share our anticipation or fear of death.

A dog crossed the road in front of my car recently who certainly had no anticipation of death. I had to help him understand this danger with my horn. When he walked calmly out in front of my car, I had to hit both the horn and the brakes. He looked up at me casually. No apparent sense of terror at a near miss.

Have you ever watched cats and mice? The popular image is of the cat stalking and the mouse terrified. But the actuality seems more like a Tom and Jerry cartoon. Though the cat may have a meal in mind, the mouse does not behave at all as a human would if stalked by a lion. It is almost as though the mouse gets into a game with the cat of "See if you can catch me"!

The original law in nature was not tooth and claw, but a very high level of cooperation. We will talk more about animals and death later on in this chapter.

Nature Is a Harmony System

Years ago on a ministry tour in my home country of New Zealand, I passed the shop of a taxidermist, a person who stuffs fish and animals for a living. I have never seen a taxidermy store before or since. He had a window display—a single, shocking exhibit. Two squirrels in this window had been killed and mounted. One squirrel was posed lying on his back, eyes open, chest blown open by a shotgun blast. The other squirrel was mounted standing with one paw resting on the other squirrel, wearing a little hunter's cap and carrying a little cocked shotgun.

When I first looked at it I laughed. Then I thought about it. If this scenario had actually taken place, something frightening would have taken place in the animal kingdom.

Why was this diorama shocking? Because despite all the PBS specials showing the violence of a hunt and the old adage "Nature red in tooth and claw," the animal kingdom does not behave as terribly as its appointed ruler.

The early chapters of Genesis (some of which we looked at in chapter 2) reveal the roots of the reason earth has experienced a multiplication of tragedy. Nowadays human beings do not only kill one another out of jealousy or rage, as Cain killed Abel; they often kill the rest of creation, too—not for self-protection or survival but just for fun.

The Cuddly Koala

Take, for example, the Australian koala. He is my all-time favorite animal. If there are animals in heaven, I will recognize my bungalow because koalas will be hanging all over it.

Koalas do nothing significant; they just sit up in trees and have little koalas, about one every other year. They eat only one food—eucalyptus leaves, about three pounds a day. They need at least eleven different kinds of gum leaves in their diet of the 600 species of eucalyptus to stay alive and healthy.

The koala is a great creature to pet because, unlike almost any other creature, he does not smell like an animal. That eucalyptus oil in the leaves goes right through his fur to his skin, so he is like a perfumed teddy bear (even though he is not a bear but a marsupial).

For a while koalas were in danger of being exterminated. Why? Because when "protector and defender man" came along, the koalas did not run away, and he liked their looks and shot them right out of the trees. For fur. For target practice. For fun.

Now steps have been taken to shelter koalas, because koalas are cute and everybody hates to lose such a unique and cuddly creature.

Morally Mad

But the koala is not alone in being at risk. Some of his late and less familiar friends have not fared nearly so well under the hand of a world ruled by Man Gone Mad. Some scholars estimate that, from environmental damage and poor land use patterns alone, by the year 2000 we will lose an average of one hundred species a day. Right now we lose at least *one thousand species a year*. Exterminated. Gone totally. Wiped out.

Mankind, given all this power to rule and subdue, has gone morally mad. In addition to his broken relationship with the Creator, he has broken harmony with the creation, and sin has introduced a run of disaster in the world. No wonder God put "fear and dread" of mankind in the animals' hearts after the destruction of the first world by flood (Genesis 9:2)! Without wariness of man the destroyer, many of the creatures we see and know would have been gone long ago. Many of the wonderfully varied animals we enjoy today might have long since been erased from the earth.

Contrast this behavior with what one observer reported when he saw a gazelle trapped in the water. A tigress went in after it, pulled it out, then dumped it on the river bank alive and left. For future food, of course? Then again, maybe not.

Nature Untouched

Silence

Nature in the raw, fallen though it is, is not as violent as nature hurt by sinful men and women. Hunters who come into areas of wildlife untouched by man find an odd thing. They remark on the incredible sense of peace and quietness they find, so tangible they may catch themselves speaking in whispers, just as when you enter the quiet sanctuary of an immense and ancient church. In fact, these hunters have reported behaving like people who have indeed stumbled into an immense cathedral filled with the presence of God.

Charles Darwin remarked:

No man can stand in the tropic forests without feeling that they are temples filled with the various productions of the God of nature, and that there is more in man than the breath of his body.[2]

Innocence

When the great naturalist professor J. D. Dana was on his voyage in the South Pacific, he beached on one of the coral islands never before visited by man.

He went ashore in the early morning and beheld a scene of tropic loveliness, brilliant with beauty and abounding in life. A great flock of tall white birds was on the beach, and as he walked towards them they looked at him with no fear and with nothing but a gentle curiosity.

They had never been frightened by powder and the deadly sting of a bullet. They knew nothing of the cruelty of man. He walked among them and placed his hands upon their tall, downy heads and necks, and stroked them as if they were pets in his own family.

Then he planned to kill one and take it home for his museum; and selecting his victim, he took out his penknife and, stroking the head of the beautiful bird, pressed the keen point through the white plumage into the neck until the feathers were spotted with a single drop of blood. The bird turned his head and looked into the great naturalist's eyes with an almost human gaze of wonder and appeal. The knife was withdrawn. A deep fountain of love and pity opened in the good man's soul and he turned away and left these innocent, unfrightened creatures of God unharmed.[3]

What must it have been like to live in the original Garden that was the still center of the Maker's wheeling rapture in creation? We have almost no sense of original nature free of the ravaging consequences of fear and greed and guilt.

Buckner also wrote:

We call animals "wild" because they are intelligent enough to keep out of the reach of man who has become their worst enemy. If they have never been mistreated, they will soon learn not to fear him. Deer, antelope, buffalo, swan, squirrels and many other animals wild in their native state placed in a park and treated kindly will soon become tame and gentle and seem to enjoy man's society. Fish that flee from the approach or even the shadow of man can be tamed and become so confiding they will approach the edge of the water and take food out of man's hand. . . . The Golden Rule will work in most cases with animals as well as man. All successful tamers of ferocious as well as domestic animals are men who treat them with perfect kindness.[4]

Animals in Cages Get into Rages

Oh, we study animals, all right. We are acknowledged experts in their life cycles, mating habits, feeding, living and dying, and the significance of these activities as applied to human beings. But time after time we draw our conclusions from captive creatures treated like mere biochemical machines with interesting DNA mixes and geophysically determined attributes.

If you were a mechanistic zoologist who believed that all life is rooted in randomness, nothing more than chemical reaction, how would you study? Capture some animals, imprison them in a cage and then watch them? Take copious notes of the creatures' ongoing reactions? "These species are fighting and are probably going to kill each other."

If I put *you* in a cage for two or three years, how would you behave? No wonder some of these captive animals fall into all kinds of strange behavior! Animals in cages seem to get into rages. What is not learned or programmed into them they seem to pick up. At times they even reflect the lifestyle and personal attitudes of their captors.

But when you go out of your safe lab into the wild to observe animals untouched by man, you find yourself shocked. Why? Because rarely in real life do you find the "abhorrent" behavior you find in the lab. Time and time again harmony proves to be *not the exception but the general rule.*

The Law of the Jungle

Charles Darwin did not believe that nature as part of God's creation once existed in tremendous cooperative harmony. He made many studies during and after his voyage on the *Beagle* and adopted a theory in light of the variations he saw. But the mindset behind his theory was adopted not from firsthand observation of nature but from an armchair theoretician named Malthus.

Malthus was a mathematician. He was bothered about why people are miserable in crowded conditions and beat up on each other. On the basis of conjecture and mathematics, Malthus came up with a population theory of life's ongoing "struggle for survival," the one Darwin adopted.

Darwin called it "the doctrine of Malthus applied with man-ifold force to the whole animal and vegetable kingdoms."[5] Later Hitler and Marx adopted the same premise, applying it (with equally radical results) to the human race.

We call now "the law of the jungle" what Herbert Spencer called *the survival of the fittest.* This is the theory that the driv-ing force behind life is only statistical survival, that all of nature is out for itself and that the "Power" (as Darwin fondly capital-ized it) of nature is individual antagonism toward the rest of the world in which various life forms compete for food.

This theory is so well-known, so overused and even so cliched that it comes as a surprise to discover that such a rule in nature did not originally even exist.

Malthus Was Misinformed

It is true, of course, that nature produces many more seeds or creatures of a species than actually survive. All of nature is linked by food chains in which lower forms of life support higher forms dependent on living provision. Darwin was right, more-over, in noting that "every being . . . must suffer destruction during some period of its life," and that if Malthus was correct "on the principle of geometrical increase, its numbers would become so inordinately great that no country could support the product."[6]

But this does not demand a "struggle for existence" of indi-viduals with one another, with different species and with the phys-ical conditions of life. That is an *assumption,* not a conclusion—something read into the data, like the fish and the submarine we looked at in chapter 3, and not implicit in the facts. (With a sim-ilar assumption, a statistician near Darwin's time predicted that the roads of the America of our time would now be completely covered by a layer of horse manure several feet thick!)

The idea actually assumes what it seeks to prove—that life is driven only by chemical selfishness and greed. No one has author-ity to supervise the chain, allocate resources and make sure every-thing is fair. All creation will always "seek its own way" regardless of the life or happiness of any other creature with which it shares resources. In short, Darwin's theory is a good description of what man looks like divorced from God. But is this the way nature is? And is it the way nature was created to be?

It's Not Nice to Fool with Mother Nature

There are records of great ferociousness among animals, not only toward humans but toward each other. Sometimes people look at one animal stalking another animal and think, "If there is a God of love and kindness, then why do foxes get into henhouses and rip those hens up? What kind of God designs a fox like that?"

But who says foxes were designed like that? Fallen man does terrifying, shocking and unimaginable things, but the Bible record shows us that these things are not part of the original pattern. Such atrocity does not prove the design is flawed; it merely shows that the product is being criminally misused.

Nor do we know whether the fox itself has been deceived. When animals get around people, they pick up the smell of people. And there may be something about the scent of human beings, especially fallen human beings, that freaks out normal animals. A fox who sees a hen who smells like a person can become one crazy fox.

It is clear to me, in any case, that nature shares in the Fall more deeply than we have explored.

Nature Takes Revenge

Do you remember how many "nature revenge" movies there were in the '60s and early '70s? *The Birds, The Attack of the Killer Bees, Them* and, of course, *Jaws.* More recently we had *Cujo, Arachnophobia,* and *Jurassic Park.* "Nature-gone-wrong" movies are the scariest movies in the world. "We're small and unnoticed now," the wronged creatures seem to say, "but we won't put up with your constant abuse. You may have forgotten what you did, but we haven't. We're coming back—and we're bad." Nature on a rampage.

But what is the actual record in unmolested nature? The rule is still often not struggle but harmony, not continual conflict but largely cooperation. Even in life-and-death situations there is alliance among the animals.

Let me offer a few examples also from Arthur Custance's studies.[7]

The Crocodile and the Zic-Zac

Crocodiles seem to have no great dream in life but to lie like logs and eat things. Since crocodiles do not floss (the last dentist they visited was lucky to get away alive), they get meat particles and little bugs in their teeth that drive them crazy.

The croc in Africa uses the services of the zic-zac, a little bird, a species of plover, who lives among the crocodiles. The crocodile opens his mouth and makes a peculiar noise that attracts the zic-zac, who flies inside the crocodile's mouth. Then the crocodile closes his mouth. But get this: He doesn't eat the bird! The bird in the darkness buzzes around inside the croc's gums and eats all the grubs, cleaning them out like a living toothpick. When he finishes dinner, he taps on the crocodile's inner mouth. The croc opens his mouth and the zic-zac flies away.

Zic-zacs also ride on the backs of crocs picking parasites from their hides where their croc hosts cannot reach.

The so-called law of the jungle says that the croc should finish each visit with zic-zac dessert. The law of God in nature, however, is harmony, and the croc and zic-zac hit it off well.

Coral and Plankton

Then there is the balance between corals and plankton. Like plants, plankton supply oxygen to corals, requiring in turn the carbonic acid produced by the little coral animals.

If the corals were to get too productive, the water would become alkaline and kill them. If the little plants got too prolific, they would be killed by their own acidity. So they all just figure things out. The plankton even adjust their levels in the water according to the light in order to harmonize.

Animals and Death

When you abuse not only the environment but your own place and responsibility in it, you affect the original purpose, the finely balanced, cooperative functioning of nature.

Preparing for Winter

The native American Indians, with their profound experiential knowledge of the ways of nature, got an idea of the severity of the coming winter by watching how hard the chipmunks and squirrels worked. If they were really into it, the Indians knew it was going to be a tough winter. But how did these furry little critters know?

Arthur Custance mentioned this to a skeptical friend of his as evidence of the design of God in nature. His friend replied, in effect, "Too bad God didn't give them more brains. Those little suckers may gather but they forget where they've hidden things. They gather all those seeds and nuts and promptly lose half of them! Stupid. If there is a God who really designs things, how come they forget?"

"But," responded Custance on reflection, "do they really forget?" Chipmunks can plant up to 17,000 trees per acre from the nuts and seeds they "forget"!

Our materialistic mindset with its presuppositions (glasses on the mind) reads into how God has structured nature but often proves utterly wrong. We assume in other life forms the experiences of our own, and impress reactions onto the animal kingdom that may not be there at all.

The fear of death is an example. Animals apparently fear pain and the unusual, but the anticipatory fear of death that we generally infer has never been proven in any animal. Animals, like the dog I mentioned at the beginning of this chapter, do not seem to anticipate death at all. When an animal dies of old age, it does not groan, start breathing fast and look terrified; it is gone, just like that. ". . .The spirit shall return unto God who gave it" (Ecclesiastes 12:7).

Dumbfounding Disney

When I think about animals' so-called death struggles, I remember one of Walt Disney's early film series, a pioneer effort in nature entertainment documentaries. You have seen footage of lions stalking game filmed through the telephoto lenses of cinematographers hidden in game blinds. There are the wildebeests looking out for the threat. Here it comes! Now they run away (with terror music dubbed in as the soundtrack) until the hunting cat jumps on one.

The Disney filmmakers' angle was to portray the fright of the game in their terrified flight from death. But as the crews were shooting the footage, they saw something that astonished them.

The prey did indeed spot the charging big cats. They did indeed run. It looked like an Olympic sprint as the whole herd got into the act. Then, in one frighteningly short, efficient stroke, the cat tagged one of the slow guys and dispatched it with a few quick, well-placed bites. But was the flight of the wildebeests really fear?

Here is the strange thing. The moment the cat actually got one, the remaining beasts stopped running and went back to eating. It was as if they were saying, "Too bad, old Jack didn't make it this time. Oh well, it was fun while it lasted." Some even stopped near their fallen mate in apparent unconcern as it was being made into lunch by the lion. Because the lion had done lunch already and he would not be needing them?

Psalm 104:21 says, "The young lions roar after their prey, and seek their meat from God."

Animals and Suffering

When one animal kills another for food or self-preservation, we may wonder, Where is the love of God in animal suffering?

But even Darwin noted that

98

when we reflect on this struggle, we may console ourselves with the full belief that the war of nature is not incessant, that no fear is felt, that death is generally prompt and that the vigorous, the healthy, the happy survive and multiply.[8]

Some unusual things have been recorded over recent years that make us rethink our assumptions about animal prey and suffering.

Surviving Tiger Attacks

Some people have survived being seized by tigers, bears or panthers. Such animals normally chew your brains out fast, yet an astonishing 64 of 66 people who survived that terrifying situation said something like this: "The moment the animal actually bit me, I felt no fear."

They were, of course, utterly shocked: "This thing is chewing my arm off while I am calmly observing!" But no fear. Many said, too, that apart from the blow or force of the bite, they had no primary perception of pain. It was as though they had been given some sort of psychic anesthetic.

What Do Animals Feel?

Perhaps the lack of anticipation of death, along with the actual numbing effect of the killing blow, makes for much less suffering in animal death than humans imagine.

Sundar Singh, the great Indian sage and Christian who was seen to walk with wild animals, commented:

All living creatures suffer in proportion to the development of their organs of sense, but not to the degree of man whose feelings and higher intellectual powers add immensity to his capacity for suffering, because whenever he imagines he has pain, his actual sufferings are increased to that extent.

Usually the teeth, claws and beaks of birds and beasts of prey are such that it is scarcely possible for the victims to escape them, so the prey is killed at once without excessive pain and saved from the suffering that would follow were it

99

to escape wounded. Then again the poison of snakes and venomous insects gets into the blood and causes such numbness that death ensues without pain.

In nature, except in a few extraordinary circumstances, death usually occurs without any excessive pain, because at the time of death the victims are only semi-conscious, either through the effect of the poison or from the shock of the wound. In short, their state is really not as evil as we often imagine it to be, but pain and suffering that are the result of either physical or spiritual evil is indeed agonizing.[9]

Surprising Scenarios

Custance relates that in Tashkent the Russians planned to shoot a nature film. Because they had little chance of coming across a deer and panther in mortal combat, they caught a panther, put him into a cage and put a captured deer into the cage with him. With cameras running, they prepared to film the panther first terrifying, then killing the helpless deer.

But something went wrong. The deer did not cooperate. Instead he figured out a great game—chasing the panther around and around the cage. The panther freaked out and finally died. An autopsy postulated a heart attack. An artificial situation indeed, but not an outcome that anybody expected.

Then there is the wasp who paralyzes a beetle in which she then lays her eggs—another incredible situation Custance records. There is no place you can touch the beetle, encased in armor, except one place, the very place the wasp stings—true with only a few species of beetle in the world. And the spot is just deep enough for the wasp stinger and paralytic ganglia to reach.

The scientist studying this phenomenon tried to find another way to paralyze the beetle but could not do it without killing the beetle outright. The wasp is apparently the only creature exactly equipped to do it.

From the moment it happens, the beetle is alive but unable to move. The wasp then lays her eggs in the beetle's body.

Although the beetle will not live to see them born, it will remain in a state of suspended animation without decaying as fresh food for the next generation of wasps.

Even amid all the violence of the hunt and the struggle for food and preservation, the dominant and original law of nature is harmony.

8

Animals: Creation
Songs of Praise

T'would ring the bells of Heaven
The wildest peal for years,
If Parson lost his senses
And people came to theirs,
And he and they together
Knelt down with angry prayers
For tamed and shabby tigers
And dancing dogs and bears,
And wretched, blind pit ponies,
And little hunted hares.

Ralph Hodgson

Robert Louis Stevenson was remonstrating with a man in the
street ill-treating a dog.

"What business is it of yours?" the man said. "He ain't
your dog."

"No, but he's God's dog," said Stevenson, "and I'm here
to protect him."

Electronic Dictionary of Quotations

Nor am I greatly moved by jocular enquiries such as: "Where
will you put all the mosquitoes?"—a question to be answered
on its own level by pointing out that if worst came to the
worst, a heaven for mosquitoes and and a hell for men could
very conveniently be combined.

C. S. Lewis

Praise Is for the Birds

Among the stories of St. Francis of Assisi is a lovely account
in Arnaldo Fortini's biography of the monk's twilight duet with
a nightingale in the woodlands of Porziuncola. As Francis and
his traveling companion, Leo, were about to eat, they heard the
bird singing in a nearby tree.

> "Let us go praise God together," says Francis, "with our
> Brother Nightingale."
>
> "I do not have a good voice," responds Leo. "You have a
> good voice and know so many beautiful songs. You must reply
> to the nightingale."
>
> And so begins a tenzon, or competitition, in the perfect
> style of Provencal troubadours—Francis and the nightingale,
> the man who had once led serenades through the streets of
> Assisi and the noble virtuoso of the woods. Which songs new
> and old does the minstrel of God bring back from his heart's
> depths to compete in this new court of love? . . .
>
> The nightingale replies. He sighs in sympathy. . . . He exults
> in a joyful song of love won again. He grows humble and plain-
> tive in prayer. He puts questions in his turn. Then he launches
> into a dizzying flood of nimble notes that rise and fall in a
> thousand tones, in a thousand swift and resonant progressions,
> in an immense jubilation that no one could resist sharing. And
> when the last passionate note dies away, everything remains
> still under the power and sweetness of that song.
>
> Francis turns to Leo and says: "Brother, truthfully I must
> confess that the nightingale has beaten me." They return to
> their meal. *The nightingale comes to rest on Francis's hand.* . . .
> Thus all together they share the supper.[1]

Centuries later Isaac Watts penned his own hymn to sing with the birds of the woods. Without embarrassment and keying off Psalm 148, he encouraged "the sweet warblers," as Francis of Assisi had, to join with him in worship of the Maker:

> Fair songsters, come; beneath the sacred grove
> We'll sit and teach the woods our Maker's name.
> Men have forgot His works, His power, His love,
> Forgot the mighty arm that reared their wondrous frame.
> Had I ten thousand hearts, my God, my Love,
> Had I ten thousand voices, all are Thine.
> Where love enflames the soul, the lips must move;
> Nor shall the song be mortal where the theme's Divine.[2]

Much Scripture is foundational to Isaac Watts' admonition to the birds to "let our different notes in praise conspire." Nor is praise just for the birds:

> Praise the Lord from the earth . . . beasts, and all cattle; creeping things, and flying fowl. . . . Let every thing that hath breath praise the Lord.
>
> Psalm 148:7, 10; 150:6a

E. D. Buckner, referring to these Scriptures nearly a century ago, wrote:

> The animate and inanimate creation all contribute to the true worship of God. All of creation must worship at whatever level of sentience they possess. Jesus said if men held back their praise, even the stones might "cry out" in worship.[3]

Israel, Showplace of Creation

Even a cursory glance shows Scripture to be filled with allusions to nature. It celebrates the position in creation of animals, plants, birds and insects. Before we explore the place of animals in the Bible, let's see how the people who lived in Bible lands viewed God's creation.

Few Westerners are aware of how rich a mix of life there is even today in the tiny geographical area of Israel. It is uniquely designed in the world as a creation showplace in order to demonstrate the creativity of God.

Lance Lambert points out that because Israel links three continents, it is a meeting ground for plants, animals, insects and birds from places as diverse as Siberia, Western Europe, inner Asia and North and East Africa.

Plants

"No other land," Lambert writes, "has a wealth of plant life within so small an area as Israel."[4] This small country has some 3,000 species of plants, compared to 1,800 species in Britain (which is two and a half times larger) and 1,500 species in Egypt (ten times larger and the site of one of the most fertile areas in the Middle East, the Nile Delta). Israel is the "eastern limit for many of the Mediterranean plants, the western limit for Asian steppe land plants, the northernmost extremity of African plants and the southernmost extremity of the eastern Siberian plants."[5]

Birds

Bird life in Israel is also remarkable, with some 450 species. Israel is the crossroads of migrant bird paths from lands as diverse as Russia's far north; Lapland or Greenland; East, Central or even South Africa.

Animals and Insects

And while animals as diverse as the African lion, the rhinoceros, hippopotamus, crocodile, Syrian bear and cheetah have now all died out, there are still "leopards, lynxes and jungle cats, ibex, gazelles and wild goats, hyenas, jackals and wolves, foxes, wild boar, porcupines, badgers and polecats."[6] (Israel seems to be the only country in the Middle East, apart from Jordan, trying to preserve the wildlife of the land.)

There are more than eighty species of reptile alone, including

the tortoise and turtle of which there are seven species; the lizards ranging from the chameleon and gecko to the desert monitor which can grow up to four feet long; and snakes of which there are at least 35 different species.... Some of these reptile species are almost extinct in the rest of the world, while the presence of others is quite remarkable.[7]

Insect life is astonishing, with invertebrates numbering in the tens of thousands.

Fish

Even the fish are unique, for this "region is a meeting place not only for continents but of seas as well!" The coral reef of the Gulf of Eilat is one of the three richest in the world, with a "vast variety of tropical fish and organisms connected with coral," for they

include the whole range of the highly diversified world of the Indo-Pacific coral reef. And since the Suez Canal was opened more than a century ago, over 200 species of tropical marine life have migrated from the Red Sea into the Mediterranean.[8]

Lambert concludes: "Add to this the remarkable range of scenery within so small an area and it becomes the cause for greatest wonder."[9]

The Land

The very land itself, in its harsh splendor, preached to the men and women of Bible times. They learned that triumph comes by trust, that life goes on after the storm, that you can reap a harvest of things you can neither see nor understand.

As godly men and women saw the living creation around them filled with wonders, they understood something wonderful about the God who placed them there. As Job observed:

Ask now the beasts, and they shall teach thee; and the fowls
of the air, and they shall tell thee: or speak to the earth, and
it shall teach thee: and the fishes of the sea shall declare unto
thee.

Job 12:7–8

The plants in Israel thus served as preachers. The insects
were sermons. Everyone who saw an eagle in the air or a fish
bright and swift in the water learned something about the ways
of wisdom. And every child with a pet lamb might learn a profound and painful lesson about love and sin and sacrifice.

God's Forgotten Friends

Dr. E. D. Buckner's book, written near the turn of the century when animal welfare and the cruel practices of vivisection
were a center of political controversy, bears an impressive title:
*The Immortality of Animals and the Relation of Man as Guardian
from a Biblical and Philosophical Hypothesis.*

The author echoed the concern felt by many as animals were
mistreated, not only in their labor in human service, but as the
subject of medical tests. (These have come into concerned focus
again today. Some lines of makeup and body lotions succeed by
being marketed as *Not Tested on Animals.*) Buckner attempted,
with other Christians of his time, to restore a biblical perspective to the place of mankind in creation:

> Viewing [God] as the Creator of all living things and seeing
> that the whole of creation is constructed upon a plan of benev-
> olence and justice, we expand to loftier, more generous and
> more holy emotions as we feel we are only part of a system,
> much of which has not been revealed.[10]

Seeing as God Sees

The root of the mistreatment of creation is the loss of biblical perspective. Treat a man or a woman as a "thing" and you
cannot fail to hurt him or her. Treat an animal as the blind prod-

uct of time, chance and matter, having no value or purpose, and you eliminate a sense of respect, love and belonging.

During the reign of Hitler, Nazi soldiers came to a hospital helmed by a Lutheran doctor. They were intent on clearing the beds for their wounded by killing the helpless patients in his care. Since there was no hope of their recovery, the soldiers felt, these patients were useless and ought to be replaced by those who could be helped.

The doctor barred them at the hospital door. His only argument was this: "These men are made in the image of God."

Men and women have meaning and value and purpose even without the ability to contribute. The Bible is clear on this. People have souls. But what does the Bible say about the rest of God's creation?

"Living Souls"

The Hebrew word for "soul," *nephesh*, is used 393 times. Properly it means "a breathing creature"—i.e., any "animal." In the abstract it means "vitality." *Nephesh* is used widely in a literal, accommodated or figurative (bodily or mental) sense. It has many meanings, including appetite, beast, body, breath and creature. Biblically, then, the soul is simply the life of a breathing creature, which departs when that living creation dies.

In Elijah's time a boy died of sunstroke. Elijah prayed for the child's resurrection and God raised him to life:

> He stretched himself upon the child three times, and cried unto the LORD, and said, O LORD my God, I pray thee, let this child's soul come into him again. And the LORD heard the voice of Elijah; and the soul of the child came into him again, and he revived.
>
> 1 Kings 17:21–22

The words "living soul" (*nephesh chayah*) were used in Genesis 2:7 when God originally gave life to man. You can read the same phrase in twelve more passages in Hebrew where, surprisingly, they all refer to animals! The first five appear in the first two chapters of Genesis:

1. Let the waters bring forth abundantly the moving creature that hath [a living soul].

Genesis 1:20

2. And God created great whales, and every living [soul] that moveth, which the waters brought forth abundantly, after their kind, and every winged fowl after his kind: and God saw that it was good (verse 21).

3. And God said, Let the earth bring forth the living [soul] after his kind, cattle, and creeping thing, and beast of the earth after his kind: and it was so (verse 24).

4. To every beast of the earth, and to every fowl of the air, and to every thing that creepeth upon the earth, wherein there is [a living soul] (verse 30).

5. And out of the ground the LORD God formed every beast of the field, and every fowl of the air; and brought them unto Adam to see what he would call them: and whatsoever Adam called every living [soul], that was the name thereof.

Genesis 2:19

The use of *soul* does not equate animals metaphysically with people. Human beings are created uniquely *in God's image,* a phrase never used of any other creature. When mankind behaves subnormally, he is compared with the "beasts that perish" (Psalm 49:12–13, 20).

But the use of *soul* does underline this: Animals have value, dignity and rights all their own as creatures of God. "A righteous man regardeth the life of his beast" (Proverbs 12:10). Animals are not made simply for the amusement or service of mankind. They have their own purposes and destiny under their Creator.

And how does God view these wonderful and complex creatures? After the first terrifying judgment of the world, God established a covenant with Noah and his sons

> 6. And with every living [soul] that is with you, of the fowl, of the cattle, and of every beast of the earth with you; from all that go out of the ark, to every beast of the earth.
>
> Genesis 9:10

> 7. God said, This is the token of the covenant which I make between me and you and every living [soul] that is with you, for perpetual generations (verse 12).

> 8. I will remember my covenant, which is between me and you and every living [soul] of all flesh; and the waters shall no more become a flood to destroy all flesh (verse 15).

> 9. And the bow shall be in the cloud; and I will look upon it, that I may remember the everlasting covenant between God and every living [soul] of all flesh that is upon the earth (verse 16).

Referring to clean and unclean foods, God calls the animate creation "souls":

> 10. This is the law of the beasts, and of the fowl, and of every living [soul] that moveth in the waters, and of every [soul] that creepeth upon the earth.
>
> Leviticus 11:46

Tributes were paid to the priest not only for the souls of men but for those of animals:

> 11. And levy a tribute unto the LORD of the men of war which went out to battle: one soul of five hundred, both of the persons, and of the beeves [cattle], and of the asses, and of the sheep.
>
> Numbers 31:28

111

The blood of certain animals was accepted as a life-for-life substitute for the life of a human being in the atonement: "The life of the flesh is in the blood: and I have given it to you upon the altar to make an atonement for your souls: for it is the blood that maketh an atonement for the soul" (Leviticus 17:11).

Finally, God said He holds the souls of all living creatures in His hands:

> 12. In whose hand is the soul of every living thing, and the breath of all mankind.
>
> Job 12:10

The Old Testament is filled with examples of God working with, by and through trees, fish, birds and animals. Dogs, lions and locusts accomplish His will. Plants are His parables. He speaks in the sound of the moving in the mulberry trees, visits Abraham under the tree at Mamre, visits Gideon under the oak at Ophrah, talks to Moses through a burning bush. He uses birds to feed the hunted prophet Elijah, a fish to preach to the runaway prophet Jonah and even an ass to speak to the wayward prophet Baalam.

Christ, the Animals' Friend

When we come to the New Testament, the link continues. The most significant parable in the New Testament, the one to which more space is allotted than any other, is the Parable of the Sower. It concerns plants as parables of lives that do or do not make it spiritually. In each case it is the condition of the soil, its proper preparation and its care that determine the ultimate destiny of the plant. Man's spiritual survival is thus linked parabolically to the condition of the earth.

New Testament Pictures

The sound of a cock crowing breaks Peter's arrogant denial and sends him weeping and penitent out into the night.

Jesus rides a humble donkey into Jerusalem, an achingly sweet revelation of God's care for a creature made the butt of jokes for centuries. G. K. Chesterton's famous children's poem "The Donkey" captures it:

> With monstrous head and sickening cry,
> And ears like errant wings;
> The devil's walking parody
> Of all four-footed things.
>
> Fools! I also had my hour;
> One far fierce hour and sweet:
> There was a shout about my ears,
> And palms before my feet.

Even the "lilies of the field" that perish are arrayed more beautifully than Solomon in all his splendor, by a God who loves beauty and joy and is willing to bestow it even on a creation that cannot last long. Jesus spoke of the sparrows being noticed and cared for by the Father, who is also aware of homes for the foxes and nests for the birds.

Jesus compared Himself to "a hen [who] gathereth her chickens under her wings" (Matthew 23:37). He is depicted in Revelation as "the Lion of the tribe of Juda" (Revelation 5:5). He appears at the end of all things riding a white horse and leading armies on white horses (Revelation 19:11–14). And the image of Jesus as "the Lamb of God which taketh away the sin of the world" (John 1:29) dominates the New Testament.

The Nativity

Dr. DeWitt Talmage, the great Presbyterian pastor, commented on Christ's birth among the animals:

> Behold . . . on the first night of Christ's life God honored the animal creation. You cannot get into that Bethlehem barn without going past the camels, the mules, the dogs and the oxen. The animals of that stable heard the first cry of the

113

infant Lord. Some of the old painters represent the oxen and camels kneeling that night before the newborn babe. And well might they kneel.

Have you ever thought that Christ came, among other things, to alleviate the sufferings of the animal creation? Was it not appropriate that He should, during the first few days and nights of His life on earth, be surrounded by the dumb beasts whose moans and plaints have for ages been a prayer to God for the arresting of their tortures and the righting of their wrongs?

It did not merely "happen" so that the unintelligent creatures of God should have been that night in close neighborhood. Not a kennel in all the centuries, not a robbed bird's nest, not a worn-out horse on the tow-path, not a herd freezing in the poorly-built cow-pen, not a freight car bringing beeves [beef] to market without water through a thousand miles of agony, not a surgeon's room witnessing the struggles of the fox or rabbit or pigeon or dog in the horrors of vivisection, but has an interest in the fact that Christ was born in a stable surrounded by animals. He remembers that night, and the prayer He heard in their pitiful moan He will answer in the punishment of those who maltreat them.[11]

Are There Animals in Heaven?

We cannot look at God's creation for long without touching on the question every child asks who has ever lost a pet: "Will I see Spot [or Puff] in heaven?" In farther-reaching terms: Does God have a purpose for the animal creation that may continue in a future life? Do the animals have any sort of destiny after death?

Numbers of Christians in the past have contributed insights on this question. John Wesley, speaking of a general restoration of all animal life, wrote:

> . . . What if it should then please the All-Gracious Creator to raise the creatures which we now call inferior animals to a higher grade in the scale of creation? What if it should please Him in the great regeneration when He makes us equal to

114

the angels to make them what we are now? Thus in that day all the vanity to which they are now helplessly subject will be abolished; they will suffer no more, either from within or without; the days of their groaning will be ended.

In the new earth as well as the new heavens, there will be nothing to give pain, but everything that the wisdom and goodness of God can create to give happiness. As a recompense for what they once suffered while under the "bondage of corruption" when God has "renewed the face of the earth" and their corruptible bodies have put on incorruption, they shall enjoy happiness suited to their state, without alloy, without interruption and without end.[12]

William Wilberforce, the Christian statesman and Member of Parliament (from 1780–1825) who labored to see the elimination of slavery in England, said in a speech before the Anti-Vivisection Society in London that he believed that

these beautiful and useful forms of life which are sometimes so cruelly tortured, are bound to pass over into another sphere, and that in that great eternal world men and animals should sink or swim together.[13]

A century ago Aggassiz, a scientist of profound religious conviction, was a firm believer in the future life of lower animals. He wrote,

Most of the arguments . . . in favor of the immortality of man apply equally to the permanency of the immortal principle in other living beings. May I not add that a future life in which man should be deprived of that great source of enjoyment and intellectual and moral improvement which result from the contemplation of the harmonies of an organic world would involve a lamentable loss; and may we not look to a spiritual concert of the combined worlds and all their inhabitants in the presence of their Creator as the highest conception of Paradise? In some incomprehensible way God Almighty has created these beings and I cannot doubt of their immortality any more than I doubt of my own.[14]

Are Our Destinies Linked?

C. S. Lewis speculated on the subject of animal immortality by considering redemption. Our own eternal destiny is dependent on our relationship to Jesus Christ. Perhaps, he believed, animal destiny is somehow linked with ours:

> If . . . the strong conviction we have of a real, though doubtless rudimentary selfhood in the higher animals and specially in those we tame is not an illusion, their destiny demands a somewhat deeper consideration. The error we must avoid is that of considering them *in themselves*. Man is to be understood only in his relation to God. The beasts are to be understood only in their relation to man, and through man to God. . . . Man was appointed by God to have dominion over the beasts, and everything a man does to an animal is either a lawful exercise or a sacrilegious abuse of an authority by divine right. . . .
>
> The theory I am suggesting . . . makes God the center of the universe and man the subordinate center of terrestrial nature; the beasts are not co-ordinate with man, but subordinate to him, and their destiny is through and through related to his. And the derivative immortality suggested for them is not a mere amende or compensation; it is part and parcel of the new heaven and the new earth, organically related to the whole suffering process of the world's fall and redemption.
>
> Supposing as I do the personality of the tame animals is largely the gift of man—that their mere sentience is reborn to soulhood in us as our mere soulhood is reborn to spirituality in Christ . . . if it is agreeable to the goodness of God that they should live again, their immortality would also be related to man—not this time to individual masters, but to humanity.[15]

Why Animals May Be Included

Dr. Buckner cites a succession of Scriptures to support his claim that animals will be included in the restoration of heaven and earth:

> The wolf also shall dwell with the lamb, and the leopard shall lie down with the kid; and the calf and the young lion and the fatling together; and a little child shall lead them. And the cow and the bear shall feed; their young ones shall lie down together. . . . And the sucking child shall play on the hole of the asp, and the weaned child shall put his hand on the cockatrice' [viper's] den.
>
> Isaiah 11:6–8

> That . . . [God] might gather together in one *all things* in Christ, both which are in heaven, and which are on earth. . . .
>
> Ephesians 1:10 (italics added)

Surrounding the throne of God in the apocalyptic vision of the apostle John were four beasts who

> give glory and honor and thanks to him that sat on the throne, who liveth for ever and ever.
>
> Revelation 4:9

As the beasts give glory to God, the twenty-four elders say,

> Thou art worthy, O Lord, to receive glory and honour and power: for thou hast created all things, and for thy pleasure they are and were created.
>
> Revelation 4:11

John saw in his vision horses, sheep, leopards, lions, frogs, fowls, birds and insects. He recorded that

> every creature which is in heaven, and on the earth, and under the earth, and such as are in the sea, and all that are in them,

heard I saying, Blessing, and honour, and glory, and power, be unto him that sitteth upon the throne, and unto the Lamb for ever and ever.

Revelation 5:13

Many of us sing the Doxology every Sunday:

> Praise God, from whom all blessings flow,
> Praise Him, all creatures here below,
> Praise Him above, ye heavenly host,
> Praise Father, Son and Holy Ghost.

Based on all these expressions of the upcoming gathering and praise of the created order, Dr. Buckner concludes,

> In the promise of "a new heaven and a new earth," God has given a plain revelation to man of the restoration of animals. In this new Garden . . . all will be restored to former harmony; there will be perpetual peace and happiness and all shall dwell together in love. The animal creation shall again gladden a new Paradise as they did when Adam and Eve called them by name, and caressed them and mingled in their society.
>
> The Bible everywhere indicates that the new earth will be a counterpart of the old before the fall, so we must conclude that lower animals who were created before man and have been his companions before and since the fall will be restored with him in the "new Creation."[16]

So What About Spot?

We find no teaching in the Bible on the future of animal life apart from the general truth that God loves all His creation. He who made them originally to bring happiness, not only to us but to Him (and to the rest of the creation), will do justly and righteously. As the creation was subject to mankind who fell, taking that creation with him, so in Christ's resurrection nature itself is caught up in human redemption. Then we shall see the world with new eyes, as God Himself sees it.

Gerard Manley Hopkins, the nineteenth-century poet who was also a Jesuit priest, wrote in "God's Grandeur" after describing mankind's pollution:

> And for all this, nature is never spent;
>   There lives the dearest freshness deep down things;
> And though the last lights off the black West went
>   Oh, morning, at the brown brink eastward, springs—
> Because the Holy Ghost over the bent
>   World broods with warm breast and with ah! bright wings.[17]

9

Cleve Backster
and His Potted Plants

Every flower of the field, every fibre of a plant, every particle
of an insect carries with it the impress of its Maker and can—
if duely considered—read us lectures of ethics or divinity.

Thomas Pope Blount

Some years ago a man named Cleve Backster headed a New
York institute specializing in polygraph work. His expertise
helped to formulate specialized procedures for accurate measurement in the field for U.S. government police and security
agencies like the C.I.A.

Lie detectors work like this: If you tell a lie and feel guilt,
your body usually "freaks out." Tiny FM micro-modulations in
your voice change when you are under stress. You start sweating
slightly, your pulse quickens, your skin resistance drops, your
mouth becomes drier and other weird things happen. These
changes in resistance in one of the "arms" of what they call in

electronics a balanced bridge circuit create a large output for a recording machine. Why does it work? Because you were not designed for falsehood, and when you lie, your whole body testifies against you.

The Plant and the Polygraph

In February 1966, Backster accidentally conducted a life-changing experiment. He had on his desk a little potted "dragon tree" rubber plant, his secretary's *dracaena massangeana*. How long does it take, he wondered, for water to get from the root system of such a plant up to the top of one of its leaves?

Backster knew that a polygraph measurement would probably show him. It can sense even a tiny drop in leaf resistance as more conductive water moves into it. And as a lie detector authority, Backster had very sensitive polygraphs.

He hooked up his secretary's plant to a polygraph and figured that when he switched it on, he would get a gradient that he could measure. This plotted line would rise slowly as the absorbed water lowered the plant leaf resistance. On the basis of that change, plotted against time, he could figure out how long it takes for water to reach the leaves of the rubber plant from the root system via the stems.

But instead of getting a straight line, what he got on his polygraph was a wavering, up-and-down, varying-resistance response line—the same sort of line that results when you hook up a person to a polygraph.

At first Backster thought the contacts were not on tightly enough. So he tightened the connections on the leaf. But the wavering went on. Then he wondered if the plant was reacting to something, like the temperature of its environment. So he got a pot of stale coffee, took another unconnected leaf and dunked it in carefully. The plant reponse plot appeared to change a bit in its reaction, but not much.

Maybe warm coffee is not a strong enough stimulus, he reasoned. *I'll get a match and burn it.*

The Shock

That very instant, something shocking happened. The line on the polygraph jumped, just as it does when a subject under examination is put under stress.

What was really shocking was this: Backster did not actually burn the plant; he simply intended to. But the plant had apparently reacted instantaneously to the *intent* of threat or harm.

Of course, Backster did not think that was what happened. Neither would you. He was sure there must be another, simpler explanation. When you are in charge of a significant institute, you do not run out into the streets shouting, "My plant just read my mind!" (You *can*, of course, but then they might put you into a room with your rubber plant and rubber wallpaper where you get to feed the birds on the calendar for a very long time.)

So you would probably do what Backster did—assume you are mistaken, that it could not possibly be true. So he repeated the experiment with other plants in many different ways. He used all kinds of checks and screens to isolate the real cause of the reaction and avoid the stunning possibility of any connection between a human thought and a plant's response.

The Backster Effect

But after many days of repeated experiments, Cleve Backster was forced to what seemed a wholly incredible conclusion that changed his life—that this simple potted plant had responded in a measurable way to his bare intention of harm toward it.

He discovered what he believed to be a mysterious connection, not apparently part of the normal electromagnetic spectrum, between living things and human beings. This form of "primary perception" is now called by some in his honor the Backster Effect.

He was finally convinced, after he automated the test process fully, removing as far as possible any alternate stimuli, that if living things get hurt or die, other living things around them usually react, sometimes violently.

The Brine Dump Experiment

Backster's proof culminated in what is now called the Brine Dump Experiment. His staff took live saltwater shrimp and connected their containers to computers able to send signals at random intervals. In another room they hooked up plants to a separate recording system. It had its own timing clocks and polygraph equipment and even used a different power supply.

They started both systems. At humanly unknown and unpredictable intervals, the computer-activated devices opened the containers randomly and dropped the shrimp into boiling water, where they died almost instantly. Every time the shrimp in the first system died, the plants in the other room reacted.

Backster has since done hundreds of experiments. More than seven thousand scientists and two dozen American universities have requested reprints of his research. His conclusion is astounding: Living things apparently react to other living things.

All Living Things React

The effect first confirmed in sensitive plants like the rubber plant and philodendron is not unique to them. It can apparently be found in all living things. Fresh fruit and vegetables react, mold, yeast, yogurt, amoeba and paramecia, blood, even cell scrapings from the roof of your mouth. So if you crack a fertile egg in your pan for breakfast, does the parsley in your refrigerator know when it dies? And if this is true, should you swear off eating entirely or cutting anything in your garden?

Let me hasten to assure you that even if it is, you can still eat a tomato or mow the lawn. The tomato gets incorporated into a much more awesome being such as yourself, and the lawn needs a good mow like a haircut.

The Bible teaches clearly, as we have already seen, that such assimilation or control is part of the created mandate on lower life forms. The so-called "food chain" was established by divine wisdom for the nurture and care of progressively higher life, and culminates in provision for human beings as the earth-keepers under God. Wise culling or cropping does not bring apparent distress to the creation.

But that is not all Backster said he discovered.

Plants Have a Memory

Backster's research has even more mind-boggling implications. What if in the future you see this scenario?

Mr. Green

A Mr. Green is being cross-examined on a witness stand. He was the only witness in the room when someone shot the pianist to death.

The prosecutor announces, "We are going to bring three men into this courtroom. We have already established that you, Mr. Green, were at the scene of the crime. Indicate to us which one of the three men was in that room when the victim was shot."

The jury is properly astonished because Mr. Green is a potted plant that sat on the piano! It is hooked up to a polygraph.

One by one they bring in the three men. When the third one walks in, the plant registers violently. They have their man.

A Plant Can Remember

In one of Cleve Backster's experiments, a plant hooked up to a polygraph acts as witness while someone walks up to another plant near it and rips it to pieces. The "recording" plant predictably reacts to the other plant's death. Later, other men come back into the room one at a time. Nothing registers. But when the man walks in who killed the first plant, the recording plant reacts violently.

Which means this: If true, even a simple plant has some sort of memory. It will not easily forget what it has seen in your actions, even in your intentions! Even the plants remember who

125

did wrong. Gardens remember cruelty. Trees record rapes. Jungles memorize murders—and murderers.

The reverse is probably also true: Plants respond to and remember kindness. Perhaps this is the secret of those gardeners who have the proverbial green thumb—the ability to help make anything grow well. Perhaps they love their plants and love their work, and the plants, like the rest of God's creation, respond in kind. If you are a Christian, your cabbages ought to know it.

Is This for Real?

Backster's work has had its criticisms, of course. Some later researchers, attempting to repeat the original experiments with even tighter controls, were unable to duplicate what he recorded. They attributed the apparent initial reaction of his plants to possible imperfect contact, or delayed surface drying effects on electrode connections.[1] Backster remains stubbornly impenitent and continues to maintain his position. He insists that plants will not perform on demand like chemical machines. To many such evidence is at best highly debatable, and anything unable to be repeated precisely at will certainly cannot be accepted as any kind of law. Other point out that even if there was any kind of reaction, we cannot say there is necessarily any kind of one-to-one correspondence between plant responses and human feelings.

This is understandable. Even if a discovery like Backster's was easy to verify, it still would not fit readily into the commonly accepted structure of reality to which we in the West are accustomed. Like parallel studies of the effects of prayer or various kinds of music on plants, reports like this seem to most of us the stuff of either blatant "inquiring-minds-want-to-know" sensationalism, "meditate-on-Shirley-MacLaine's-navel" mysticism, or just plain science fiction.

Nor are studies in areas like this without danger. People who conduct such experiments are often either without a biblically informed view of the world, or they have in some way strayed spiritually into the fringes of the occult and psychic.

Even Backster himself has not always been able to repeat his results, but does not feel these exceptions disprove his discovery. On the contrary, he believes that plants, like people and animals, do not behave like mere machines with simple automated electrochemical reponses that are always identical. He believes that plants, like the rest of the living creation, get hurt, tired, afraid and abused and sometimes refuse to respond on demand to an uncaring experimenter's wishes.

Try It Yourself!

You can, of course, seek to verify some of his discoveries for yourself (as G. De La Waar reported in *Electro Technology* magazine, "Do Plants Feel Emotion?", April 1969) without access to the expensive, original electronics of Backster's first polygraphs.

The basic element of his test equipment, a simple op-amp balanced bridge resistance circuit, can be duplicated cheaply, so that people with a modicum of electronics skill can try it themselves. (See "Experimental Electroculture" by George Lawrence, *Popular Electronics*, February 1971; and for a schematic diagram and parts list, "More Experiments in Electroculture," June 1971, pp. 63–68, 93. See also articles in *Electronics World*, October 1969, pp. 2–28, and April 1970, pp. 27–29.)

Chart recorders to register responses, once very expensive, are now much cheaper, and you might substitute a borrowed oscilloscope and videocamera for recording. For plant connections, instead of the contacts of the original experiments, try the stick-on disposable conductive electrodes that hospitals use.

The Impact of Death

Backster, at least, was wholly convinced he was onto something awesome. His comments, when the first implications of his discovery broke on him, are significant.

Plants subjected continually to the hurt or shock of the death of other plants nearby—or living creatures like the shrimp—

eventually did not respond well. They had in some way become inured and no longer reacted strongly to the loss of life. But Backster said the one thing his plants never seemed to get used to—and this was the part of his early research that moved him the most—was the effect on plants of the death of something human (even blood cells). The reaction was always the same: intense agitation.

The Voice of Blood

While a reporter was visiting Backster in his lab, Backster noticed that the pen recorder connected to the plant was reacting violently to something. Yet to his mind neither he nor the reporter was doing or intending anything that would be perceived by the plant as harmful.

Puzzled, Backster searched for a possible reason for the agitated response and found it: The reporter was picking absentmindedly at a small scab on his hand. Some fresh blood cells under the scab were dying. Those dying human cells were apparently communicating a powerful, painful message to the plant.

Blood "Crying Out"

Does this sound familiar? After Cain killed Abel, God said to him,

> What hast thou done? the voice of thy brother's blood crieth unto me from the ground.
>
> Genesis 4:10

Perhaps what we think is only biblical poetry is actuality. We saw in the last chapter that our blood, according to Scripture, is the "life of the flesh" (Leviticus 17:11; see also Deuteronomy 12:23).

Loren Eisley, the anthropologist, recalled a time when he fell and gashed his head, and some of his blood spilled onto the sidewalk where he had fallen:

Confused, painfully, I murmured, "Oh, don't go. I'm sorry." The words were spoken to no one but to a part of myself. I was quite sane, only it was an oddly detached sanity, for I was addressing blood cells, phagocytes, platelets, all the crawling, living independent wonders that had been part of me, and now through my folly and lack of care were dying like beached fish on the hot pavement. I was made up of millions of these tiny creatures, their toil, their sacrifice, as they hurried to seal and repair the rent fabric of this vast being whom they had unknowingly, but in love, compounded. I was their galaxy, their creation. For the first time, I loved them consciously. It seemed to me then, as it does now in retrospect, that I had caused to the Universe I inhabited as many deaths as the explosion of a supernova in the cosmos.[2]

"What have you done?" said God to Cain. "The voice of your brother's blood cries out to Me from the ground."

It was this realization that deeply touched Cleve Backster. Based on what the death of just a few human blood cells did to his agonized plant, think of what a cry of agony must go up from a jungle or a forest in a time of war!

"[They] shed innocent blood," said God in sorrow over a generation that killed its own children. It offered them on the altar of Molech in exchange for the promise of wealth, pleasure and power,

> even the blood of their sons and of their daughters, whom they sacrificed unto the idols of Canaan: and the land was polluted with blood.
>
> Psalm 106:38

Pollution of the Land

The Hebrew word for *polluted, chaneph,* means "straying from God's right path." *Transgressing His laws, violating His statutes and breaking His covenant* all contribute to the pollution of the land, points out *The Hebrew-Greek Study Bible,* citing Isaiah 24:5 and Jeremiah 3:1–2. Specifically identified as polluting is *murder* (Numbers 35:33).

Millions of dying cells, one hundred trillion voices speak in each unique individual human body. Every time a human being dies, it is like the death of the very representative of God to the cells of the creation composing us.

Jesus said of the Pharisees that He sent them prophets

"That upon you may come all the righteous blood shed upon the earth, from the blood of righteous Abel unto the blood of Zacharias son of Barachias, whom ye slew between the temple and the altar."

Matthew 23:35

Backster, while not a Christian, summed it up like this:

This whole thing has made me a believer in prayer. If one cell communicates like this to another, what is the effect of a whole multitude crying out?[3]

Does the Earth "Hurt"?

Alice Walker, an ecological feminist, sees nature responding to our environmental offenses as a species:

Just as human beings perceive all trees as one . . . all human beings to the trees are one. We are judged by our worst collective behavior since it is so vast, not by our best. The earth holds us responsible for our crimes against it not as individuals but as a species. . . . I found [this] to be a terrifying thought.[4]

Now listen to the prophet Jeremiah:

How long shall the land mourn, and the herbs of every field wither, for the wickedness of them that dwell therein? the

beasts are consumed, and the birds; because they said, He
shall not see our last end.

Jeremiah 12:4

Is it possible that we live among a hurting creation literally
mourning the sin of mankind? Does the earth itself actually
weep over what man in sin is doing to the creation, to each other,
to God?

Job, arguing his own righteousness, said:

If my land cry against me, or that the furrows likewise thereof
complain; let thistles grow instead of wheat, and cockle
instead of barley.

Job 31:38, 40

More than Metaphor?

The word *cry out* here, according to *The Greek-Hebrew Study
Bible*, is *za'aq*—to shriek from anguish or a sense of danger. It is
a distress signal.

We have no direct warrant from Backster's experiments alone
to say that a plant response has any direct parallel to human feelings or human hurt. Backster's evidence may indeed not be con-
clusive or valid and he may be a sincerely mistaken man who
risked his career and reputation on something unproven by his
equipment and unprovable by anything in our present technology. What he claims may not be what he actually recorded, and
skeptics may be wholly justified in dismissing his discovery.

What is important to you and me is that despite our ability
or inability to establish such links in a lab, a great part of the
non-Western world historically and even today lives out its life
on the basis that such a reality exists. We may dismiss this as fantasy if we are materialists, or as cultural religious deception if we
are missionaries and properly aware of the dangers of pantheism, monism, and demonism. But we cannot ignore the fact that
in the world view of the Bible, at least part of what Backster
claims is true. If the language of some Scripture is more than

131

metaphor, it declares with great force that the land itself hurts and grieves over the sin of man.

> They have made it desolate, and being desolate it mourneth unto me; the whole land is made desolate, because no man layeth it to heart.
>
> Jeremiah 12:11

The word *desolate* here (*shamem*) means to stun, grow numb, devastate, stupefy; to be astonished, appalled, ravaged, wasted, destitute. That verb is used ninety times in the Old Testament. It is used to describe Tamar after she was raped by Absalom (2 Samuel 13:20). Again from *The Greek-Hebrew Study Bible*: "It is something so horrible that it can leave a person speechless."[5] No wonder the consequence of national wrong is national judgment that strikes directly at the life support of mankind itself!

"The field is wasted, the land mourneth," wrote the prophet, seeing the terror to come, "for the corn is wasted: the new wine is dried up, the oil languisheth" (Joel 1:10).

The connection between the desolation of the land due to human sin and the crying out of the land to God might offer an interesting biblical parallel to Cleve Backster's strange discovery. What if these passages are true *literally* and his findings are, as he claims to have demonstrated to himself beyond reasonable doubt, utterly true?

Is all creation in some mysterious way linked? And what is the link?

The Mysterious Link

Backster said that when he felt a sense of personal apprehension, such as when his arriving plane was touching down, his assistants back in the lab could sometimes tell the exact time of landing based on the response record of his plants.

We do not know what such a connection between human and plants might be. We do not know whether it could be something measurable as a new form of energy, or something beyond the electromagnetic—a new spectrum no one has yet explored. Some will surely see parallels with the new pictures of the universe that the worlds of quantum physics, relativity and holographics have opened up to us in recent years. Time will tell.

But all creation shares in something. Not some common, random-caused, genetic ancestry like the West's fiction of macro-evolution. Not the East's vision of some common "ground of being." What if its secret is instead the consequence of *being a living co-creation under God*, implying a common spiritual perception of well-being or intended harm?

On a simple perceptual level, what if even the surrounding environment is linked by an *innate knowledge of good or evil, right or wrong*? What if all the created world, had we eyes to see, is unanimous in encouraging choices for virtue and reacting against wickedness? What if, in other words, the Bible is *literally* true when it says, "The whole creation groaneth and travaileth in pain," waiting "for the manifestation of the sons of God" (Romans 8:22, 19)?

What Have We Lost?

Most of those in the two-thirds world share a deeper appreciation than we do of creation. John Mbiti says that to many of the African peoples, nothing sorrowful happens by accident or chance; it all must be caused by some agent, either human or spiritual:

> Some societies think a person suffers because he has contravened some regulation, and God or the spirits therefore punish the offender. . . . But in most cases different forms of suffering are believed to be caused by human agents. . . . In the experience of evil, African peoples see certain individuals as being intricately involved, but wickedly in the otherwise smooth running of the natural universe.[6]

In Scripture we find (as we have already seen), a fundamental basis for sympathy, understanding and care for *all* of creation.

This is neither Western rationalistic ("We are all chemicals") nor New Age pantheistic ("We are all god"), and it is much more profound than some "He ain't heavy, he's my brother" ditty.

Early Primal Perception

The early Christians, I believe, understood the importance of the care of creation. Certainly not on the technological level we might now, but innately, because they lived in a culture with closer ties to nature and a sense of the supernatural. People groups whose primary lifestyle is agricultural, who set their time sense more by sunsets and sunrises than clocks, feel constant dependence for their very lives.

It is this sense of dependence, of needing help outside ourselves, that is largely missing in the Western world. When your very survival is vulnerable to situations beyond your control, situations like drought or flood or insect plague, you stay humbled under the mercy of God.

Here is a question to consider: If even "dumb" little potted plants are linked with other created life, might it hold true all the way up? Perhaps it is mankind who by the Fall has lost touch with something that the whole creation around him to some degree still shares.

After all, originally we made the wrong moral choice, and the consequences of our action spilled over into the rest of the creation. We are told God Himself brought a curse on the ground. This may not only limit man's leisure time to sin, but protect the earth itself, much as God put a fear of man into the animals after the Fall to protect them from being wiped out. Perhaps nature originally owned or enjoyed something that since the Fall has been suppressed or hidden for its own protection.

Animal Sensitivity to the Spiritual World

Animals may perceive the spiritual world more clearly than rebellious man. In many places the Bible makes this plain. The account of Balaam and his ass, which we mentioned in the last chapter, is an obvious example: The ass saw the angel sent to judge Balaam before the prophet did (Numbers 22:21–35). Here the ass remembered her history with Balaam, made a righteous decision based on the fear of God, and rebuked the madness of the prophet. We might notice that the Bible does not say God "spoke through" the ass, but rather that He "opened her mouth" and she spoke. Of course, this was a special case. But what if all animals before the Fall could talk?

We looked, too, at when God commanded the ravens to feed Elijah, and the whale to swallow Jonah. God even sent a plant, then a worm to eat that plant, whose subsequent death brought Jonah a godly perspective on the revival in Nineveh.

Daniel, cast into a den of lions, was spared because the lions recognized and responded to an angelic protector: "My God hath sent his angel, and hath shut the lions' mouths, that they have not hurt me" (Daniel 6:22).

Seeing the Spiritual

Domestic animals like cats and dogs often know instinctively when spiritual entities are in the room, sometimes when human beings seem to have little or no idea at all. Even in my own limited experience I have seen unusual reactions from animals—personal pets caught inadvertently in some situation when they saw something apparently supernatural that humans in the same room had not yet recognized, and slinked out of the room in great distress.

One of the most astonishing things my wife Fae and I ever witnessed was during our visit one Sabbath evening to the Wailing Wall in Jerusalem as guests of the Billy Graham organization. Standing on the hill overlooking the square from which the wall rises, we saw a group of young rabbinical students welcoming an old, obviously much-loved and revered rabbi. They helped him out of his taxi. To our surprise and delight, they broke into a spontaneous circling dance, holding hands around him.

Then we saw what apparently no one else saw. In the sky immediately above them, high above the square, *a flock of birds circled in time with the students,* looking for all the world, to Fae and me, as though they were joining in with the worship of their Creator.

No Wildness

We discussed in chapter 1 that Christians of previous centuries were more alive to the presence of God in nature. In the last chapter we saw St. Francis of Assisi enjoining the birds of the woods to join him in worship of the Maker, who actually did. In these birds and animals, who recognize in such men and women the touch of God, is no wildness. It is as if they are saying, "I'm not afraid of you because you belong to God."

The famous account of St. Francis meeting with a killer wolf and subduing it only by preaching, and the record of men like Sundar Singh who was able to talk to and pet predator cats, seem to most of us the stuff of exaggeration or fables. After all, animals cannot respond to the Holy Spirit!

But both history and Scripture indicate otherwise.

The Supernatural Basis of Ecology

What do we find in the actual records of Scripture? Read these verses with me from Paul's letter to the Romans and ask yourself this question: When we talk about redemption, why do we think only of us?

> I reckon that the sufferings of this present time are not worthy to be compared with the glory which shall be revealed in us. For the earnest expectation of the creature waiteth for the manifestation of the sons of God. For the creature was made subject to vanity [NIV, *subjected to frustration*], not willingly, but by reason of him who hath subjected the same in hope, because the creature itself also shall be delivered from the bondage of corruption into the glorious liberty of the children of God. For we know that the whole creation groaneth and travaileth in pain together until now.
>
> Romans 8:18–22

Much more than humanity is hurt by human sin, and that "other" happiness is tied up wholly with ours.

I hope you are beginning to look with new eyes at this familiar passage, which lays a biblical foundation for the connectedness of created life and the participation of nature in the coming redemption. (We will look again at this passage in chapter 11, and in more detail in Appendix 1 on p. 181.)

What Will Bring Healing?

I am convinced that the more we understand the wonder of God's world, the more we will understand just how deep is its hurt. When mankind first sinned, creation fell with him. What will bring healing to this poor, abused creation? The restoration of the original. The return of God's keeper to his rightful spiritual place. "The manifestation of the sons of God."

None of us acts in isolation. "No man," wrote the Christian poet John Donne, "is an island." People may say they believe in doing their own thing as long as it doesn't hurt anyone. But sin always hurts someone, and that hurt may be bigger than any of us imagine. When you sin, you do not just sin against yourself. Nor do you sin just against your relationships or against society. You sin against the very core of creation around you. Your wrong affects everything.

What, after all, is our "environment"? Paulus Mar Gregorios of the Indian Orthodox Church comments on the implications of the relation of the Godhead to the creation:

> Neither art nor literature, neither mountain nor river, neither flower nor field came into existence without Christ and the Holy Spirit. They exist now because they are sustained by God. The creative energy of God is the true (sustaining) being of all that is; matter is that spirit or energy in physical form. Therefore we should regard our human environment as the energy of God in a form that is accessible to our senses.[7]

No wonder sin is directed ultimately against God! It will all come to light. Everything covered shall be revealed, and what we have done to hurt the world will not be covered forever. The very living world around knows when we are wrong, and you may "be sure your sin will find you out" (Numbers 32:23).

The implication of the passage in Romans is astonishing. It says that *the environment itself is waiting for people's conversions, for revival.* The ecology needs the impact of world evangelization. God's whole creation looks forward to His raising up the people who love Him, His restoring us to our proper place as God's servants, to heal the hurt of the world.

What I hope to show you in Part 3 is the Bible's vision of a supernatural Christian ecology—a whole new basis for loving our world.

Part **3**

Healing the Land

I saw God wash the world last night.
Ah, would He had washed me. . . .

William L. Stidger

The Christian who believes the Bible should be the person who . . . is treating nature now in the direction of the way nature will be then. . . . God's calling to the Christian now and to the Christian community in the area of nature . . . is that we should exhibit now a substantial healing between man and nature and nature and itself as far as Christians can bring it to pass.

Francis Schaeffer

10

Four Judgments
of God on a Land

Yea, as I walk through the valley of death,
I shall fear no evil,
For the valleys are gone
And only death awaits
And I am the evil.

Robert Lifton
Home from the War

Fly away, Peter, fly away, Paul,
Before there's nothing left to fly away at all;
Take to the sky, higher than high,
Before the silv'ry rain begins to fall.

Cliff Richard
"Silvery Rain"

In the early nineteenth century, a large meteor shower filled
the night skies above Europe with an awesome display of shooting stars. High-altitude dust scattering through the atmosphere
made the full moon that night look as if it had been dipped in

blood. People in many cities who saw it fell on their faces in repentance, convinced that the end of the world had come.

Which comes first, revival or judgment? God speaks His Word by prophets or preachers, but what if they are silent or men and women do not listen? What happens when human sin pushes divine mercy to the limits of wisdom?

The Four Judgments

Ezekiel 14 records four judgments that God warns will visit an offending land:

+● **Famine:** "Son of man, if a country sins against me by being unfaithful and I stretch out my hand against it to cut off its food supply and send famine upon it and kill its men and their animals . . ." (verse 13, NIV).

+● **Ecological Devastation:** "Or if I send wild beasts through that country and they leave it childless and it becomes desolate so that no one can pass through it because of the beasts . . ." (verse 15).

+● **War:** "Or if I bring a sword against that country and say, 'Let the sword pass throughout the land,' and I kill its men and their animals . . ." (verse 17).

+● **Disease:** "Or if I send a plague into that land and pour out my wrath upon it through bloodshed, killing its men and their animals, as surely as I live, declares the Sovereign LORD, even if Noah, Daniel and Job were in it, they could save neither son nor daughter. They would save only themselves by their righteousness" (verses 19–20).

Famine. Ecological devastation. War. Disease. Four prophetic voices designed to get our attention when our moral madness is full. What we do not want to acknowledge will not be overlooked: that we cannot get away with living as if God does not exist or as if He has nothing to say to us.

Economic Pinch

Economic crisis is linked biblically to the misplaced focus of our lives—maintaining our own "houses" to the detriment of God's house:

> Ye looked for much, and, lo, it came to little; and when ye bought it home, I did blow upon it. Why? saith the LORD of hosts. Because of mine house that is waste, and ye run every man unto his own house. Therefore the heaven over you is stayed from dew, and the earth is stayed from her fruit.
>
> Haggai 1:9–10

It is no secret that the Western world faces a staggering economic burden. The causes are many, the warnings dire, the consequences frightening. Yet the root cause is none of the usual factors on which we usually lay blame. The root cause is *moral*. The source: personal selfishness, greed and carelessness.

The Sermons of Nature

The same four judgments as in Ezekiel face the last generation of mankind:

> I looked, and behold a pale horse: and his name that sat on him was Death, and Hell followed with him. And power was given unto them over the fourth part of the earth, to kill with sword, and with hunger, and with death, and with the beasts of the earth.
>
> Revelation 6:8

Look at the plain record of history. When men and women forget God, tragedies multiply until we are brought face to face with either destruction or salvation. The psalmist, in describing God's dealings with His people, wrote that "he called down famine on the land and destroyed all their supplies of food" (Psalm 105:16, NIV).

Over the centuries God has rebuked our rebellion and immorality by the sermons of the crops, the weather, the "dogs of war" and the removal of His hand of protection from the ravages of disease. If you sin against God, even nature will turn against you.

The Core of Environmental Apathy

> I call heaven and earth to record this day against you, that I have set before you life and death, blessing and cursing: therefore choose life, that both thou and thy seed may live.
>
> Deuteronomy 30:19

With these solemn words, Joshua faced Israel with a choice: *Live or die.* Like a legal record in a modern courtroom, that significant choice today has a global and cosmic witness: the heavens and the earth.

But most of us are not listening, to God or to the signs around us in the earth. Ecologists themselves face constantly the frustration of audience apathy. What is the point of marshaling all kinds of facts if people no longer listen? What good is it to warn people about imminent danger if they don't even care?

The syndrome is not unique to the threat of environmental extinction. We have become like a generation that plans its picnics on the slopes of a rumbling Mount St. Helens, partygoers on the eve of Hurricane Andrew. Even if the warnings are true, we are not that interested.

The Theological Key

William H. Becker links our apathy about the current ecological crisis with a neglected theological key: the implications of the Fall and the consequences of original sin. He says:

> We may recycle . . . and take proper satisfaction for doing so, but we remain caught in a web of [sinful] spiritual assumptions abut success and consumption, progress and waste that effectively undermine and trivialize our efforts to escape.[1]

The whole of the Western world is eaten out with a sense of its own supreme importance and self-confidence. Like Belteshazzar of old, we have taken the holy cups from the Lord's sanctuary and filled them with Babylonian beer to blow the froth off into God's face.

Westerners may make commercials about preserving Walden Pond, identify with the Green Movement and sing about loving and taking care of the planet, yet all the while continue with a lifestyle that is utterly destructive. Like a fish in the water that does not really understand what "wetness" is, we cannot see without a massive change of perception just how much we ourselves are the key part of the problem.

Writes Becker:

> The tendency towards estrangement and self-destructive choices is an inescapable given of human existence. Sin is chosen (otherwise it would simply be necessary evil) and the choice is central to the very identity of the chooser. But the choice is made in a social context that predetermines its direction. "The historic dimension of estrangement," as Langdon Gilkey says, "is passed on communally. We absorb more than our cultural ethos—language, concepts, norms and so on—from our own heritage; we absorb also that community's fallen character—its centering of its world on itself, its inordinate self-love and love of its own."
>
> The doctrine of original sin helps us see we are socializing ourselves to sin ecologically.[2]

How can God shake us out of our moral stupor? What will get our attention and make us realize just how far from reality we have come in our sin?

A Sense of Place

The very first thing we miss when we turn from God is a sense of belonging, as Michael W. Smith sings in his American

Music Award-winning song "A Place in This World." Having no place to belong is one of the most devastating situations in life.

> By the rivers of Babylon, there we sat down, yea, we wept, when we remembered Zion.
>
> Psalm 137:1

Linked with Land

A sense of belonging is linked intimately with the land. As Walter Brueggemann observes in his landmark study, *The Land*:

> It is now clear that a sense of place is a human hunger which the urban promise has not met. And a fresh look at the Bible suggests that a sense of place is a primary category of faith. . . . It is rootlessness and not meaninglessness which characterizes the current crisis. There are no meanings apart from roots. . . .
>
> Place is space with historic meaning where some things have happened which are now remembered and which provide continuity and identity across the generations. Place is space in which important words have been spoken, which have established identity, defined vocation and envisioned destiny. . . . Vows have been exchanged, promises made, demands issued. Place is a protest against the unpromising pursuit of space. It is a declaration that our humanness cannot be found in escape, detachment, absence of commitment and undefined freedom.[3]

Having a sense of place is conditional. (We will look at the three main conditions in the next section.)

Israel was promised land by God for her future identity and inheritance so long as she was true to Him. If she remained faithful, she would not have to be sojourners forever like Abraham "looking for a country," wanderers like those who died in the "long, dusty death of the desert" without entering the Land of Promise, exiles like those of the captivity in Babylon.

When the Land Is Judged

The first consequence of judged land is crop failure and economic disaster. Imagine what the following judgments did to the Israelites' sense of place:

> I called for a drought upon the land, and upon the mountains, and upon the corn, and upon the new wine, and upon the oil, and upon that which the ground bringeth forth, and upon men, and upon cattle, and upon all the labor of the hands.
>
> Haggai 1:11

> And then the Lord's wrath be kindled against you, and he shut up the heaven, that there be no rain, and that the land yield not her fruit; and lest ye perish quickly from off the good land which the Lord giveth you.
>
> Deuteronomy 11:17

> All thy trees and fruit of thy land shall the locust consume.
>
> Deuteronomy 28:42

> And your strength shall be spent in vain: for your land shall not yield her increase, neither shall the trees of the land yield their fruits.
>
> Leviticus 26:20

Touch the land and you touch mankind. Not until the land itself begins to fail do people begin to realize that something is badly wrong.

A Recent Example

Charles Lynn, a "voice crying in the wilderness" to key agriculturalists and industrialists, describes the Dust Bowl crisis in the Midwest during the Great Depression:

> In 1930 wheat farmers experienced a large decreased yield per acre. The cattle industry had great difficulty due to dry grazing land. A rainfall at harvest helped to ease the problem,

but when the crop was harvested, the prices of wheat were greatly reduced because of the Depression.

The drought resumed again in 1932 with record-breaking temperatures although, due to troubles throughout the United States, the Plains farmers' woes seemed insignificant to many in the industrialized East. Not only did the soil shift and die, but approximately 300 deaths from heat occurred in Kansas alone in 1934. Dust choked out the greenery and the term *dust pneumonia* was coined for any respiratory problem. Town people dependent on agriculture were less motivated to stay as farmers went West. Some scholars say the dust bowl crisis caused the migration Westward.

The eyes of the seers and prophets seemed closed at this time, but where they failed, ministers and minstrels chronicled the events by songs that rang out over the land and caused many to heed the crisis in rural America.[4]

What are the implications from the 1930s for our own time and place? Concludes Lynn:

> America cannot shrug off another drought and trust in technology instead of rain to deliver our fields. We can marvel that the Scripture gives us Elijah as a model to set our sights on in prayer. A man or a people that can open or shut the windows of heaven is of utmost importance to a nation's life, economy and existence.[5]

Conditions for Keeping the Land

It is one thing to have land. It is something else to keep it and be blessed by it. Land can create its own set of temptations. Having it can be as big a problem as not having it. Walter Brueggemann identifies the central temptation of land:

> It seems to contain in its own gifts adequate means to secure existence. The sources of fertility are in the land itself . . . and the gods who claim these gifts are subject to manipulation, ready to serve human ends of satiation. As everything else in

this consciousness, so these gods; everything is put at disposal, usable for self-security.[6]

Three Conditions

You may have land and a place to belong, God says, on three conditions:

◄▶ **Fidelity:** Do not give yourself to idolatry.

◄▶ **Gratitude:** Always remember that everything you have is a gift.

◄▶ **Compassion:** Take care of those in covenant with you who have neither the power nor the ability to take care of themselves and who have no legal claim or power to land: the poor (Exodus 23:6; Deuteronomy 15:7–11); the stranger who comes to live among you (Exodus 22:21; 23:9; Deuteronomy 10:19); the Levite (Deuteronomy 14:27, 29); the widow and orphan (Exodus 22:22–24; Deuteronomy 14:29).

Rejection of Idolatry

This is why the most serious and primary command given to Israel was the prohibition of idols and the rejection of idol worship. Idolatry for Hebrew believers was not a religious option, nor was accommodation to any form of false worship. They knew their very lives depended on implicit obedience to God's revealed laws.

But we can easily begin to put our trust in the creation and not the Creator; to look to the land and not to the Lord for our provision.

An idol or image, according to Brueggemann, is a "controllable representation of our best loyalties and visions," an effort "to reduce to manageable and predictable forms the sources of value and power in our lives." We begin by making up our own gods; we end when they, invested with the demonic, begin to

149

rule us instead. Ancient images became not only frightening but deadly.

The eventual idolatry that ruled the ancient world was the worship of gods made in the most violent likeness of nature and man. The ancient terrors of Baal and Molech, Ashera and Ashteroth first ruled the cycles of the seasons; ultimately they demanded the life of a nation's children to guarantee its future fertility.

What Brueggemann observes of Israel is true today of the Western world. Our central temptation, he writes, is (like that of ancient Israel) to "forget and so cease to be a historical people open either to the Lord of history or to His blessings not yet given." God sometimes needs to shake us out of our slumber, and He often does so by dealing with the land.

Significance of the Sabbath

The Sabbath, continues Brueggemann, was a reminder "that all of life and the land was a gift from a gracious God":

> In the Sabbath, we are reminded that life does not center in getting or holding things. A halt is called to the continual commerce of covetousness; Sabbath tells us life is made for living in the joyful rest of God. That is why time and time again, especially in times of prosperity and blessing, God calls on His people not to forget Him.[7]

The Blessings of Obedience

The blessings of obedience to a nation meeting these three conditions, according to Leviticus 26, are:

⇥ **Ecological Health:** "I will give you rain in due season, and the land shall yield her increase, and the trees of the field shall yield their fruit" (verse 4).

⇥ **Economic Health:** "Ye shall eat your bread to the full, and dwell in your land safely" (verse 5).

⁍ **Personal Security:** "I will give peace in the land, and ye shall lie down, and none shall make you afraid" (verse 6a).

⁍ **Civil Security:** "I will rid evil beasts out of the land, neither shall the sword go through your land" (verse 6b).

⁍ **International Security:** "Ye shall chase your enemies, and they shall fall before you by the sword. And five of you shall chase an hundred, and an hundred of you shall put ten thousand to flight" (verses 7–8a).

⁍ **Honor and Growth:** "I will have respect unto you, and make you fruitful, and multiply you..." (verse 9).

⁍ **Innovation and Creativity:** "You will still be eating last year's harvest when you will have to move it out to make room for the new" (verse 10, NIV).

The Characteristics of Judgment

If Israel rejected God's conditions of living in the land, an ever-intensifying judgment was bound to fall on them, according to the same chapter, Leviticus 26:

⁍ **Disease:** "I will even appoint over you terror [literally *trembling*, rendered *trouble* in Psalm 78:33 and Isaiah 65:23, denoting mental anguish and anxiety], consumption [from a root signifying "to waste away"], and the burning ague [fever, from a root signifying "to kindle a fire"]" (verse 16).

⁍ **Dustbowl Soil:** "I will break the pride of your power; and I will make your heaven as iron, and your earth as brass: and your strength shall be spent in vain: for your land shall not yield her increase, neither shall the trees of the land yield their fruits" (verses 19–20).

⁍ **Destructive Ecology:** "I will also send wild beasts among you, which shall rob you of your children, and destroy your cattle, and make you few in number . . ." (verse 22; see

151

Deuteronomy 32:24; Ezekiel 5:17; 14:15; Judges 6:3–5; Isaiah 33:8).

4➤ **Disaster** by sword, disease, famine and captivity: "They that are left of you shall pine away in their iniquity in your enemies' lands" (verse 39a). This includes war, plague, economic collapse, finally even exile from the land.

4➤ **Desolation** of the entire nation: "I will bring the land into desolation: and your enemies which dwell therein shall be astonished at it" (verse 32). The imagery is terrifying: corpses piled over the ruins of the idols that proved powerless to save in the day of trouble; cannibalism even of their own children; cities in ruin; invading armies left in consternation at the destruction.

What Makes the Land Sick?

Here is the picture as God sees it of a people living in a land and ignoring His commandments:

> The land . . . is an unclean land with the filthiness of the people of the lands, with their abominations, which have filled it from one end to another with their uncleanness.
>
> Ezra 9:11

In God's eyes, sin has made the land sick. Examine the following two passages with the help of a Hebrew-Greek Study Bible and *Strong's Exhaustive Concordance*:

> The land is full of adulterers; for because of swearing the land mourneth; the pleasant places of the wilderness are dried up, and their course is evil, and their force is not right.
>
> Jeremiah 23:10

The Hebrew word for *swearing* here is *alah*, a solemn oath or promise between God and His people (e.g., Deuteronomy 29:12), and the curse for breaking this oath (e.g., Deuteronomy 29:14–21; Isaiah 24:6).

I will make the land desolate, because they have committed
a trespass, saith the Lord GOD.

Ezekiel 15:8

The word *trespass* is *ma'al*, a primary root that means to cover
up; to act secretly, treacherously. It occurs 35 times in Hebrew
and indicates the deliberate violation of religious law, directed
specifically against God (e.g., Leviticus 6:2).

The sickness of the land, then, is a direct result of not following God's conditions of living in the land.

"What Shall We Do for Our Fair Sister?"

In the final judgment, great significance is given to those
who hurt the earth:

And the nations were angry, and thy wrath is come, and the
time of the dead, that they should be judged, and that thou
shouldest give reward unto thy servants the prophets, and to
the saints, and them that fear thy name, small and great; and
shouldest destroy them which destroy the earth.

Revelation 11:18

Yet even here, earth itself is not the ultimate concern of heaven,
but the people on it. The word *ge* for *earth* is used in the Septu-
agint more than two thousand times, in the New Testament 248
times. In neither place, according to *The Dictionary of New Testament Theology*, "is there any thought of divinity about it."

Earth as used here, explains *The Hebrew-Greek Study Bible*, is

the part of creation denoting man's domain and the history
transacted between God and man. . . . The earth given man
stands in a relation of dependence to heaven which is the
dwelling-place of God (Psalm 2:4; Matthew 5:3), for which
the question always is, "How will that which occurs on earth
be estimated in heaven?" . . . Thus earth is the sphere of the
kosmos, the people dwelling on earth.[8]

Mistakes of Eco-Theology

Some eco-theologians hope to rectify our poor response to environmental issues. According to William Becker they do three things:

⚜ *They emphasize God more as Creator than Redeemer* (as Thomas Berry did, or Matthew Fox with his *Creation Spirituality*).

⚜ *They overemphasize the dignity and spirituality of the material world of creation* to correct the false assumption (viewed as Christian) that matter is somehow evil.

⚜ *They focus on mere human responsibility for ecological healing.* From Matthew Fox: "God is not going . . . to pick up the pieces and remedy the disasters we bring about."

Becker points out that would-be eco-reformers offer as transformational energizers either terror ("We are killing ourselves by pollution!") or a form of hope, perhaps in some new myth like much New Age theology, offering to "imaginatively reintegrate the human race into the rest of creation."

But neither fond hope nor fears too easy to forget is an adequate dynamic for lasting change. Both are self-centered; both may deny personal accountability for wrong.

Need for a Savior

The biblical dynamic, by contrast, is repentance:

We have willingly caused what Martin Buber called "a wound in the order of being" and healing that wound in our planet's being and in our own requires repentance. Indeed, any "terror" we feel at the threat of our own self-destruction without accompanying repentance is but a further expression of human arrogance.[9]

Neither attempt to rectify environmental wrong requires the risk of divine intervention or judgment. To fix things, we are left

154

to our own devices. All is still in our power. Yet as Becker points out (although current ecological theologians deny it angrily), ecology still needs a Savior:

> If we assume no divine Savior will intervene to undo our self-destructive ethocide, then we are faced with yet another terrifying thought: not simply that we may not be able to save the planet, but that we may not be able, truly and wholeheartedly, to will to save it. Our fundamental challenge is not simply changing our economy, but changing ourselves. Can we, given our ecological sin, muster the will to change what we are?[10]

Christ is the only true source of life that lasts forever. We need Him or we die. God is not only able to intervene in our environment; He has done so before and will do so again.

If we do not listen to the warnings of His Word, if we worship other gods that cannot save us, if we forget His benefits and live as if all we have is both earned and deserved by the power of our own hands, then we must not be surprised if the environment itself turns against our madness. If we who do have land treat those for whom we have responsibility to care as if they are without worth, and give them no place to belong, He will visit our land again in judgment. He will not be ignored.

The Ultimate Recycling

We can cry out to God for mercy, and may be encouraged by both Scripture and history to believe that God can act into our hopeless situations with healing. But even this is only temporary. Scripture speaks of a final end to rampant decay on both a global and a galactic scale. God will ultimately recycle everything except His own dear children, and even they get new bodies!

"Heaven and earth will pass away"—and it will be terrifying—but only to make way for a new heaven and a new earth (Revelation 21:1; 2 Peter 3:13). "Their passing," observes *The*

Dictionary of New Testament Theology, "means the passing away of the present sinful world order, which must be renewed by passing through God's judgments."[11]

Even in this judgment, we will see the utter greatness of God. What Jesus accomplished on the cross is more than the doorway back for lost mankind. When man sinned, the occasion of his fall was a tree, and the ground cursed brought forth thorns. When the Lord Jesus died, He died on a tree with a crown of thorns on His head, and He caught up creation's curse with our sin on the cross.

> Redemption extends to the furthest corner of the physical realm. That the "meek will inherit the earth" is the promise of Christ (Matt. 5:5), and this earthly kingdom is the same as the kingdom of heaven, the world of the coming age, the coming redeemed creation (Rom. 8:21).[12]

Even so, come, Lord Jesus.

11

Restored:
A New Heaven
and a New Earth

The end of God's creating the world was to prepare a kingdom for His Son.

Jonathan Edwards

Why have those Christian groups most concerned with evangelism, personal salvation and holy living often been last to see that reconciliation between persons and their Creator is incomplete if it does not include a reconciliation with the creation from which they are estranged?

Loren Wilkinson

I have sometimes wondered if the convulsions of nature in disasters like earthquakes, eruptions and floods are the ugly parables of her private pain. Stripped of meaning by human sin, abused continually like a mute beast of burden unable to vocalize injustice, the earth itself sometimes seems to rebel. Every now and then the land, utterly ignored, the shock of her silence accepted as consent, her tragedy taken for granted, screams out in hurt and rage.

"For three things *the earth is disquieted*," says Agur in the book of Proverbs, "and for four which it cannot bear." Then he lists four instances when someone who does not deserve either platform or privilege, rule or right, takes a place of power or prominence (Proverbs 30:21–23).

With our shocking record of lost stewardship, wasted resources and arrogance, crowned only with the heady public speech of a fool, could we blame the earth if it indeed had such a reaction?

Birth Pains in Nature

Let's look again at Romans 8:18–22, keeping in mind the promise of redemption shared with all created life:

> I reckon that the sufferings of this present time are not worthy to be compared with the glory which shall be revealed in us. For the earnest expectation of the creature waiteth for the manifestation of the sons of God. For the creature was made subject to vanity [NIV, *subjected to frustration*], not willingly, but by reason of him who hath subjected the same in hope, because the creature itself also shall be delivered from the bondage of corruption into the glorious liberty of the children of God. For we know that the whole creation groaneth and travaileth in pain together until now.
>
> Romans 8:18–22

Albert Barnes thinks that the last phrase, *We know that the whole creation groaneth and travaileth in* [or *with*] *pain together until now*, speaks of creation's testimony to mankind:

> By the words *we know* Paul appeals . . . to a Book always open to those who have eyes to read it: Nature itself, the daily sight of which proclaims loudly enough all the apostle here says.

Is there not a cry of universal suffering, a woeful sigh perpetually ascending from the whole life of nature? . . .

The preposition *with* . . . can only refer to the concurrence of all the beings of nature in this common groaning. But there is more than groaning in this case; there is effort, travail. . . . It seems as if Nature bore in her bosom the germ of a more perfect nature, and as the poet says "feels in her womb the leaping of a new universe."

The Apostle having averted to the glory that awaits the Christian . . . exalts our idea of it still higher by representing the external world as participating in it and waiting for it. "Nothing could be better adapted to this object than the grand and beautiful figure of the whole creation waiting and longing for the glorious revelation of the Son of God and the consummation of His Kingdom" (Hodge). . . . It must be understood of the whole inanimate and irrational kingdom.[1]

Creation iself, and not only men and women, experience a sense of dislocation, lostness, being cut off:

Schelling said [that] Nature with its melancholy charm resembles a bride who at the very moment when she was fully dressed for marriage, saw the bridegroom to whom she was to be united die on the day of her wedding. "She still stands with her fresh crown and in her bridal dress, but her eyes are full of tears."[2]

Healing the Land of Israel

Israel became a nation again only in 1948, recognized by the United Nations in 1949. Since that time Israelis have invested time, money, scientific skill and considerable ingenuity to get the land back on its feet, including massive replanting efforts, building desalinization plants and terracing the slopes for market gardens. In many places the land really is an example of a desert blossoming "as the rose" (Isaiah 35:1).

Yet if you had visited Israel a generation ago and taken a good look around at the land, you might be hard-pressed to understand why God had said what He did about it! It would be legitimate to ask, "Were these people so hard up for a place to stay after their long desert trek that the land just *looked* as good as milk and honey to them? Or has something changed since the time of that promise?"

A "Marginal" Land

Read the following descriptions of the land since 1948:

> [The land] was barren and largely treeless; its soils had been eroded to a point where the bareness of the underlying rock structures protruded, and everywhere could be seen the traces of former cultivation long since abandoned. . . . Much of the damage and neglect had been caused during the centuries of Arab and Turkish rule because of the attitude of these rulers to land and its use.
>
> All uncultivated lands were regarded as commons, to be grazed at will by the owners of animals; agriculture itself was not highly regarded as a way of life, and often even arable land was held common so cultivators had no incentive to improve their farming.[3]

Stuck in between deserts to the south and east and humidity to the north, Israel is, as Baly noted, "in every sense marginal land," and its occupation demands intensive care. Although we saw in chapter 8 the incredible variety of plant and animal life in Israel, the land itself may always have required care. It is neither desert nor like early Egypt; not a climate without rain nor a land based on river irrigation ensuring crop water.

One thing sure about Palestine is this: It is not a place where crops grow effortlessly! If ever a land was designed as a showcase for industry, integrity and ingenuity, Israel is it. According to *The Pictorial Encyclopedia of the Bible*,

> Its variable winter rainfall must be conserved and used wisely; its hillsides must be terraced to avoid soil loss; its vegetation

must be safeguarded or it will degenerate into scrub or bare earth.

Neglect and idleness are soon advertised by the appearance of the landscape:

> Palestine, in fact, is very much what its inhabitants make of it, and what they are making of it can be seen by all. . . . It is, in other words, an environment that encourages virtue and that advertises idleness, disobedience and [in Israel's history] lack of faith in God. It is hard to believe that His choice was a random one.[4]

The Early and Latter Rains

One of Israel's great blessings in this century is the literal fulfillment of the biblical promise of the "first rain and the latter rain," when after a hiatus of centuries, her people returned to the Land of Promise.

> The land, whither ye go to possess it, is a land of hills and valleys, and drinketh water of the rain of heaven: a land which the LORD thy God careth for: the eyes of the LORD thy God are always upon it, from the beginning of the year even unto the end of the year.
>
> And it shall come to pass, if ye shall hearken diligently unto my commandments which I command you this day, to love the LORD your God, and to serve him with all your heart and with all your soul, that I will give you the rain of your land in his due season, *the first rain and the latter rain*, that thou mayest gather in thy corn, and thy wine, and thine oil. And I will send grass in thy fields for thy cattle, that thou mayest eat and be full.
>
> Take heed to yourselves, that your heart be not deceived, and ye turn aside, and serve other gods, and worship them; and then the LORD's wrath be kindled against you, and he shut up the heaven, that there be no rain, and that the land

yield not her fruit; and lest ye perish quickly from off the good land which the LORD giveth you.

Deuteronomy 11:11–17 (italics added)

A Literal Fulfillment

Explaining the early and latter rains, symbolic of God's hand of blessing on the land, *The Pictorial Encyclopedia* points out that Israel is a land of two main seasons—hot, arid summer and cool, wet winter. Since virtually no rain falls from June to September, the two critical periods for farming are the beginning and end of the wet season, when temperatures are high enough to promote growth and the soil moist enough to till.

If the "early rain" at the start of the rainy season in October and November is delayed, the hard-baked soil cannot be plowed or sown; later crop yields will suffer. Too long a delay may mean crop failure. On the other end of the wet season, the "latter rain" in the warmth of late April and May is more valuable than the cold of January or February; every extension increases the crop yield.

It is a point of wonder to many inhabitants of the Promised Land that after centuries in which these early and latter rains in popular memory virtually ceased, the rains resumed when Israel again became a nation and they have continued. On November 23, 1949, in fact (the year Israel was officially recognized by the United Nations), a record of more than four and a half inches of rain fell in a single hour in Haifa—over 17% of the total rain in the area for a year.

Righteousness and Crop Productivity

If ye be willing and obedient, ye shall eat the good of the land.
Isaiah 1:19

Then I will give you rain in due season, and the land shall yield her increase, and the trees of the field shall yield their fruit. And your threshing shall reach unto the vintage, and the vintage shall reach unto the sowing time: and ye shall eat your bread to the full, and dwell in your land safely.

Leviticus 26:4–5

If you took on as a major project the task of comparing the prevalence of certain kinds of sin in a nation with the consequent agricultural productivity of the land, I believe you would find a real and direct correspondence. In times of spiritual awakening, when men and women turn to God in great numbers and begin to learn of His works as well as His ways, not only do their industry and innovation improve their harvests, but the land itself responds in blessing.

Biblical Blessings

The blessing of the land is linked in Scripture with obedience in keeping the land. Recall the blessings we looked at in the last chapter, and consider this sampling of promises:

◄► **Peace:** "I will give peace in the land, and ye shall lie down, and none shall make you afraid: and I will rid evil beasts out of the land, neither shall the sword go through your land" (Leviticus 26:6).

◄► **Security:** "I will make with them a covenant of peace, and will cause the evil beasts to cease out of the land: and they shall dwell safely in the wilderness, and sleep in the woods" (Ezekiel 34:25).

◄► **Fruitfulness:** "And the tree of the field shall yield her fruit, and the earth shall yield her increase, and they shall be safe in their land . . ." (verse 27).

◄► **Deliverance:** ". . . And [they] shall know that I am the LORD, when I have broken the bands of their yoke, and delivered them out of the hand of those that served themselves of them" (verse 27).

➶ **Safety:** "And they shall no more be a prey to the heathen, neither shall the beast of the land devour them; but they shall dwell safely . . ." (verse 28).

➶ **No Fear:** ". . . And none shall make them afraid" (verse 28).

➶ **Forgiveness:** "Then hear thou in heaven, and forgive the sin of thy servants, and of thy people Israel, that thou teach them the good way wherein they should walk. . . ." (1 Kings 8:36).

➶ **Rain:** ". . . And give rain upon thy land, which thou hast given to thy people for an inheritance" (verse 36).

➶ **Protection:** "If there be in the land famine, if there be pestilence, blasting, mildew, locust, or if there be caterpillar; if their enemy besiege them in the land of their cities; whatsoever plague, whatsoever sickness there be . . . hear thou . . . and forgive, and do, and give to every man according to his ways . . ." (verses 37, 39).

This is what God's Word declares, although finding ecological evidence of the reality of God's promises in the records of history or contemporary illustration, on a local or even national scale, remains almost uncharted research territory. Such a task would provide new avenues of evidence for the godly scholars, agricultural scientists and students of spiritual awakenings among us.

Land Suffers from Its People's Sin

Idolatry, covetousness and injustice will not be tolerated by God for long in a beloved land. And until these are rooted out stem and branch in a judged area, no effective long-term change will take place, despite all our technology and well-meaning efforts, in the ecosystems. Perhaps this is one great arena where we in the twentieth century are unwilling to bite the bullet and deal with the real roots of poverty, drought, famine and sickness.

When people sin and build a history of idolatry, the land itself reacts. The root causes of personal and national unrest, according to Scripture, of the loss of peace and harmony in both the moral and natural worlds, are always the same: the loss of love and wisdom, and the enthroning of selfishness and stupidity. Sometimes the wrong and ignorance that hurt a nation are its own, sometimes that of an invader, as in the greed and lust that lead to conquest or war (James 3:11–4:8). Not all disasters are directly attibutable to national idolatry, of course, just as individual hurt is not always attributable to personal sin. There are times, after all, when the "Lord was not in the wind" (1 Kings 19:11). But as long as sin ravages our nations, innocents may suffer; we cannot always avoid the consequances of wrong let loose in our world.

Take for yourself this challenge. Look at the nations of the world that suffer from the greatest poverty, drought, sickness and disease, where ecological disaster seems to be a constant curse. Then ask yourself this question: *What is the dominant religious mindset of this place?* In what ways do they mirror what the true and living God says about how to think and how to live? In what ways, ignorantly or not, are they actually seeking to follow the Truth whose ultimate expression is Jesus Christ, the Son of God, who "so loved" His world that He gave His very life for it? What has been the spiritual history of this land? What was it like before its present state? Where does it presently seem headed?

The correlations are never wholly simple, of course. We are not God and cannot see more than a fraction of what has gone on and is going on in lands that God still loves, despite even long-entrenched sin. But I believe that even a cursory comparison between the traits God says He will bless *in the land* and the traits He says He will judge *in the land* will underline the truth of the Bible: "Righteousness exalteth a nation: but sin is a reproach to any people" (Proverbs 14:34).

Notice the phrase *Righteousness [not religion] exalteth a nation.* Countries that are deeply religious have suffered terrible ecological disasters. Hinduism, for all its centuries of deep sensitivity to the spiritual, has not helped the beautiful and fertile land of India to feed her poor and minister to her outcasts. Islam's agriculturally disastrous nomadic and militant lifestyle has given it an embarrassing record of ecological mismanagement. Protestant and Roman Catholic missionaries have often been the chief culprits in hurting the very lands they have sought so zealously to liberate. Ethiopia, once one of the great Christian nations of Africa, is after toppling her leadership one of the most disastrous famine regions on the planet. Even places that return to the Lord will take time and wisdom to see healing.

But righteousness in the Bible is more than just right; it involves both revealing and admitting the truth of something, and drawing on the grace and help God provides to bring that spotlighted deviation back to normal. That is why the Great Commission given by Christ to the disciples was not only to *preach the gospel* (for a change of heart) but to *teach* or disciple all nations (for a change of understanding). The revival that brings a change of heart and attitude must be accompanied by a reformation that brings a change of mind and world view (Matthew 28:20). True Christian missions work always seeks the total welfare of the nation to which it comes. A Gospel that does not seek to meet the whole need of the whole man in the whole land is not the Gospel Jesus entrusted to His first disciples.

From a Distance

A friend of mine knows one of the team that processes data from one of the great Landsat satellites. These monitor constantly from space not only the movements of clouds and weather but, through their multi-spectrum cameras, the crops and growth on the very land masses themselves. Day by day, actual shifts on the face of nature as moved into and acted on by man can be seen as a recordable image—earth seen, as the song says, "from a distance." What we think, what we believe, what we do, makes a tangible difference to that record.

Referring to one of the dominant militant religious systems on earth, this team member commented, "You can tell where they evangelize. You can actually see it. When they move in, the land begins to die around them."

That is the record of history. One of the key centers for this religious system was once a greenbelt, a breadbasket of provision and beauty for the area. Now it is almost devoid of plant life, almost totally desert, a wasteland.

What causes this? Is it just bad land management and ignorance of natural chains? Are there purely physical causes involved here? Is it only a question of not knowing how to care for the land?

All this is, of course, true. People without skill as farmers or without access to agricultural science and technology may eventually destroy the land. But there is more to this than meets the eye.

Ideas, as we first saw in chapter 2, have spiritual consequences. The environment is affected by us even more deeply than we imagine. The Bible says the earth itself reacts to the sin or righteousness of mankind.

The land can be blessed by God:

Land that drinks in the rain often falling on it and that produces a crop useful to those for whom it is farmed receives the blessing of God.

Hebrews 6:7, NIV

The land can be cursed by man's sin:

. . . Cursed is the ground for thy sake. . . .

Genesis 3:17

"I Will Heal Your Land"

One passage speaks of divine judgment that comes because of sin:

If there be dearth in the land, if there be pestilence, if there be blasting, or mildew, locusts, or caterpillars; if their ene-

167

mies besiege them in the cities of their land; whatsoever sore or whatsoever sickness there be. . . .

2 Chronicles 6:28

The Conditions

If the people return to the true God and His ways, the land will rejoice again. Here is the heart of the verse so often quoted in the hope of spiritual awakening:

If my people, which are called by my name, shall humble themselves, and pray, and seek my face, and turn from their wicked ways. . . .

2 Chronicles 7:14

People "called by His name," who claim allegiance to the living God and not to idols, ought to know better than to participate in what God calls wickedness. The expressed conditions of this promise are *humility, prayer, earnestly crying out to God* and *repentance.*

The Promise

The consequences of such a return to righteousness is wonderful:

. . . Then will I hear from heaven, and will forgive their sin, and will heal their land (verse 14).

The Overlooked Context

Usually when we read or hear the promise that God will *heal our land,* we think He means, *Heal our people.* The primary benefit of such tearful repentance, we think, will be a restored people. And, of course, that is true.

But that is not the primary context of the blessing. Look at the verse that precedes it:

If I shut up heaven that there be no rain, or if I command the locusts to devour the land, or if I send pestilence among my people . . . (verse 13).

It is clearly an environmental, ecological text. The judgment of God for sin was against the very ecology; the curse came on the environment. "Cursed is the ground because of you," God said to Adam. Albert Wolters points out that "the very soil is affected by man's sin, making agriculture more difficult."

I will heal your land means just that—the healing of the land.

The Personal Key to Ecological Healing

Do you want to do something significant for the endangered environment? Do you want to make a real and significant difference in the world?

First of all and by all means, do all you have been urged by others who are likewise concerned about "our fair sister," the earth. Act responsibly in whatever you are empowered to change in your immediate and extended neighborhood. Support whatever efforts you can to keep the environment fresh and clean, an inheritance for your children. As Edith Schaeffer rightly observed:

A Christian who has been made in the image of God and is therefore meant to be creative on a finite level should certainly have more understanding of his responsibility to treat God's creation with sensitivity and should develop his talents to do something to beautify his little spot on the world's surface.

Neighbors, friends and strangers walking by ought to find the Christian's gardens, farms, estates, schools, hospitals, huts, missions and factories surrounded by the beauty of grass, moss, rocks, ferns, bushes, trees, flowers and vegetables planted and cared for with an expression of originality and artistic planning on some scale. A Christian organization should not move into a property and turn it into a shambles. The opposite should be true. It should grow and blossom into a place of beauty, demonstrating something of the wonder of the One who made plant life to produce seed in the first place.

Christians should have more beautiful gardens, should be more careful to build without cutting down lovely trees, should be more sensitive about keeping the brook unspoiled as it bubbles through their lands. Sadly, this has often not been so. . . . Certainly we who have a logical base for beauty as well as morals should be the ones to be fitting our landscape gardening into artistically beautiful and ecologically sound treatment of land and plants.[5]

But above all, "do the right thing" first. Do not speak of guarding a clean earth with a dirty heart and an idolatry-polluted soul. Do not ask for the blessing of heaven when you have every intention of living like hell. Get your own soul right with the living God. Get the ground of your life broken up, watered in tears, sown in righteousness. Become a man or woman God can trust with the care of His creation.

Take the hurt out of His heart and you will do far more in this first step of personal change than anything else offered you as "salvation" for our planet. The one thing you and I cannot do, He has promised to do and has literal power to do: God can heal the land.

Outback Miracle

In Adelaide a few years ago I met with another itinerant evangelist friend whose primary mission field was in the arid areas of the Australian outback. He told me about an environmental visitation that not only illustrates this promise perfectly; it has the earmarks of a miracle.

He was conducting a crusade, he told me, in a tiny farming community in the grip of a terrible drought. Year after year the rains had not come, and one by one the struggling farmers in the region had mortgaged everything they owned to keep their farms afloat and their families alive.

But now time had run out. If no rain fell again this season, the banks would foreclose and the farmers would lose everything.

In the middle of his little meeting, a delegation of these desperate men showed up. They were out of answers, out of resources, out of options. There was only one hope now for them—a miracle. So they came, all the key men, the true-blue, fair-dinkum Aussie farmers who in normal times would be tempted to think of church as something best left for children and old ladies. They came to ask God for a hand.

The evangelist was perplexed. What could he do? Then he remembered a strange incident someone had told him about. A godly woman had believed she had had a word from God to go to another small city in Australia, a city with a hard reputation spiritually, and intercede for it. The word she was given was to pray specifically over the "gates of the city."

The only trouble was, when she got there she couldn't see any "gates." Little wonder; modern cities don't have gates! Puzzled, she sought the Lord further. Then she realized what she was to do: Go down to the on-ramps and off-ramps of the major freeways into and out of the city and there offer her prayers. So this is what she did.

But she did more. She felt strongly that she should do what must have seemed to her even stranger than prayer in each of those public places. She felt she was to offer holy Communion on the very ground of each of those areas!

So she did.

And that week, beginning the day after her task was completed, she personally won more than a dozen people to Christ in the streets of that supposedly spiritually hard city.

Remembering this story, and moved by the plight of these helpless men whose very livelihoods hung in the balance, the outback evangelist led them in a simple prayer of repentance and dependence, and then began to lead them in his own little service of Communion.

"I looked outside the window," he told me later, "and the dust was swirling so thick I couldn't even see my car, though it was just a few feet from the window. And then, feeling very much like a fool, I walked out into the choking dust with the men and offered, with them, a little bit of the bread and wine to the ground outside."

171

Nothing happened. There was no lightning, no thunder. Nothing seemed to change. The men went home and the preacher finished his meeting. But within 24 hours, he said, there was such a torrent of rain in the area that it washed down top-soil from the hills and he was mudbound for the next few days, unable to leave town at all.

And as a result of that tempest of rain and mud, the farmers had a crop that year *almost three times larger* than any crop in the recorded history of the area. Their farms were saved and their families spared.

"I will heal their land."

The Restoration of Healing in History

Trace the history of spiritual awakenings down through the centuries. You will see that every revival has brought a restoration to the generation that first experienced it of just how big a concept *salvation* (or *healing* or *wholeness*) really is.

Albert Wolters points out how striking it is that most Bible words connected with salvation imply a *return* to an original good state or condition:

*Re*demption means to give back original freedom at a cost.

*Re*conciliation is for former friends or allies who have fallen out or declared war on one another.

*Re*newal means to renovate or make brand-new what has become worn or worse for wear.

*Re*generation (and all the phrases like *quicken, save, make alive, restore* that are in other places translated *revive*) imply a return to life after death.

Even the key word for salvation itself, *soteria*, was originally translated *health* in William Tyndale's 1525 New Testament (the basis of the King James Bible). This is why, observes Wolters, "theologians have sometimes spoken of salvation as 're-creation'—not to imply that God scraps His original creation and in Jesus Christ makes a new one," but suggesting that He holds onto His original fallen creation and, in the sacrificial gift of the life of His own Son, moves to save the original project.

> In a very significant sense, this restoration means that salvation does not bring anything new. Redemption is not a matter of an addition of a spiritual or supernatural dimension to creaturely life that was lacking before; rather it is a matter of bringing new life and vitality to what was there all along.[6]

Simply put, "God don't make junk" and He doesn't like to junk what He makes.

God's Unfolding Work

We can look at the whole of revival history as God's unfolding acts of mercy that progressively restore, amplify and magnify the full meaning of salvation.

In the Reformation we learned anew that *God can forgive us from our guilt*, that we can by faith be restored to peace with Him.

In the first Great Awakening under the Wesleys and George Whitefield, we learned further that He can effect the double cure: *God can heal us from the power of sin itself and from the fracture of our own personalities*, of man against himself.

The Second and Third Awakenings brought even greater light as we saw God's comprehensive provision in Christ revealed for the effects of sin on society. Here we saw the that *God can heal the divisions between man and man*, as the Gospel brought a mandate of change into society itself with its fallen structures rooted in sin.

And so it continues through the generations up until our century. The 1904 Welsh revival sent *healing worship* through the world. Azusa Street in 1906 launched the healing wave of *two-thirds world evangelization*. And the restored power of Pentecost in the healing revivals of the early part of this century revived the truth of *physical healing* to a sick and weary generation that had tried to live without miracles.

Notice that in each of these awakenings, something implicit in salvation was made explicit, something neglected made new, something already promised claimed afresh. Century after unfolding century this revelation has gone on, from strength to strength—the "old, old story" ever new.

Further notice that the scope is widening from the smaller to the greater as God unpacks His multidimensional promise in greater detail. We have seen His healing extended to families, marriages, bodies and minds.

What is it that characterizes our own day? The gifting and equipping of the Church for her final mission: *the healing of megacities and untouched peoples and nations, the mandate to tell the whole world that Christ the Savior has come.*

True but Not Exhaustive

While each of these healings is real, it is not exhaustive. A woman in Christ can be forgiven wholeheartedly, but it will not be the whole, nor the end of her forgiveness. A man can be cleansed from sin and his iniquities "remembered no more," but that cleansing does not end God's ongoing dealings in his life.

Many societies and cultures have felt the shock of true revival, but God is not finished with His world yet. You may be truly healed by Christ, but there is always provision for further help in time of need. A mind, a marriage, a family may all taste true redemption, but none ever experiences redemption in full finality. Everything God does with us in our finite, fallen world is real but not exhaustive.

And what is true with a man or a woman can likewise be true with a world.

The Final Redemption

One day—and for this we have His promise—the long process will be over. What is provisionally complete in Christ will be actually completed in His world.

174

- ❧ "The kingdoms of this world [will] become the kingdoms of our Lord, and of his Christ" (Revelation 11:15).

- ❧ We shall see no longer "through a glass, darkly; but then face to face," and know as we are known (1 Corinthians 13:12).

- ❧ "This mortal must put on immortality" (1 Corinthians 15:53).

- ❧ We will move into the house "not made with hands" (Hebrews 9:11).

- ❧ We will obtain an incorruptible crown (1 Corinthians 9:25).

- ❧ On that glad day, "every knee [shall] bow . . . and every tongue confess that Jesus Christ is Lord, to the glory of God the Father" (Philippians 2:10–11, NIV).

Where will all this take place? In the final redemption, in the focus to which the entire creation has been longing for, hoping for, waiting for: "a new heaven and a new earth" (Revelation 21:1). God has not forgotten His suffering world. One day it too shall experience its own resurrection and be born anew into a full and perfect created glory. The old earth shall pass away; all things He will make new.

How, Then, Shall We Live?

Until then, what can we do?

On the basis of what God has said, we can believe Him for some working models of redemption. We can show our poor, broken world men and women truly healed of guilt; of sin; of physical, social and emotional hurt—real but not exhaustive examples of His active grace in our lives. Not *all* men and women, but a significant number; not *all* things fully renewed but many genuinely renewed.

His grace in people. In vocations. In cultures and disciplines. In governments. In cities. In nations. And perhaps for such a time as this, we may even dare to expect from time to time what all the world longs to see—a miniature but real *healing of our planet.*

Not wholly global. Not final. Not complete. But in places determined by His wisdom and will, genuine divine intervention to break curses and judgments that have ruled for centuries, perhaps, in places that await the proclamation of His power.

The Miracle at Dunkirk

God can intervene in human history. He can do it in such obvious and powerful ways that entire nations are conscious of His dealings with them. One such intervention happened two generations ago.

Dunkirk (French, *Dunkerque*) is a port city on the North Sea coast of France seven miles from the Belgian border. Founded before the nineteenth century, Dunkirk (whose name is derived from the Flemish for *Church of the Dunes*) saw the evacuation during World War II of more than 330,000 British, French and Belgian soldiers by sea in the face of German attack. The evacuation involved Britain's national hero, Bernard Law Montgomery, popularly known as Monty. It also involved something now forgotten: that what happened there was plainly termed by those involved "a miracle."

The history books describe the evacuation:

> During the winter of 1939–40 the French army and the German Wehrmacht faced one another in what was regarded satirically as the *sitzkrieg*, or sit-down war. The world waited in anticipation of a major conflict between two powerful forces. On May 13 a bridgehead was established at Sedan, considered the gateway to France, and then suddenly, on May 16, 1940, a day after the Dutch capitulation, the German blitzkrieg was released on northern France. German mechanized forces outflanked the Maginot Line, surprised the Allies by attacking through the wooded Ardennes rather than the

Belgian plain, and drove the British Expeditionary Force (BEF) from the continent at Dunkirk.[7]

What most books do not mention is what happened to the weather that day. Around that time of year the Strait of Dover, a narrow channel at the eastern end of the English Channel between England and France, is almost always a choppy, roiling sea, making passage difficult even for large ships.

The Allied armies trapped by the Germans were forced down to the beaches of the "Church of the Dunes." With no massive numbers of backup military transport ships available, it seemed a foregone conclusion that the Germans would overrun the Allies, resulting in a terrible slaughter and total surrender. The weather was particularly bad, and unless they could get every available boat and ship across the Channel, the men were lost. The entire direction of the war hinged on what would happen next.

What is never mentioned is that England was called by radio to urgent, agonized prayer. All over England prayer went up for the men trapped there. And something happened never forgotten by the survivors of that day.

God answered prayer. A sudden fog rolled down onto Dunkirk. The seas that were always rough calmed down. And on scores of little pleasure boats, including rowboats, the Allies were evacuated safely to England.

Time rolls on and the intervention arising from intercession is forgotten. But the effect of the Allied evacuation on the nations was tangible and immediate. That day was widely called "the miracle of Dunkirk."

Weather Miracles in Iraq

I am told by a key chaplain involved in the Middle East in the winter of 1991 that a similar situation happened at the beginning of the Gulf War.

American troops preparing to launch the Desert Storm initiative against Iraq were somberly expecting the worst. Thousands of coffins and body bags had been ordered in preparation for what many believed would be one of the most terrible battles of modern times. What made it even more frightening was that the forces of Saddam Hussein were expected to use retaliatory missiles with possible poison gas or even nuclear warheads. On top of this, thousands of landmines had been buried all across the dry desert sands awaiting the attack. By all expectations, there would be a terrible cost to this conflict.

Americans were worried. Much prayer went up to God for mercy, while many felt that this war would be an occasion of judgment on the United States for her arrogance and sin.

Then, contrary to previous regulations in a strongly Muslim area, troops were allowed to have and use Bibles. Scriptures were brought by the thousands into an area that had never before allowed them. Right into the heart of the lands known in the Bible as Persia and Babylon, the ancient homes of two of the most powerful dark, spiritistic forces mentioned in Scripture, came a flood of Bibles and a bevy of soldiers suddenly, soberly interested in the things of God.

One Christian chaplain claims that thousands in the Allied armies began to turn to Christ, while much prayer went up from their home nations for the safety and protection of the troops.

And God did it again. The night before the Desert Storm offensive, *it rained.* On the morning of the offensive, that rain (so rare in a desert area) came down hard enough to expose a large number of the landmines, making it much simpler to avoid them. And the wind, which had been predictable in the past, changed direction and blew where it hardly ever did—back toward the Iraqi's own lines, making the launching of poison gas a hazard.

Most of us have seen the incredible sights of what happened over that short offensive, especially the Muslim prisoners of war falling on their knees and kissing the feet of their captors, who to their utter surprise fed and cared for them in a way wholly unlike their own Islamic bosses. The paucity of U.S. casualties and fatalities for the war was a constant source of amazement and thankfulness, even to men like General Norman Schwarzkopf who had planned the attack.

The coffins were used, all right, but many found a use no one had calculated: They became baptismal fonts for soldiers who became converts during the war!

Stories like this crop up in every war accompanied by prayer, intercession, repentance and humility. Yet this God who intervenes in weather for good can call also down judgment on a land that will not listen in exactly the same way.

Healing the Earth

Behind all the secular soothsaying and odd religious offerings we see in our day over our fragile planet, another Force is at work that transcends mere humanism and neo-pagan occultism. Perhaps there is more at work here than the Church has noticed.

Is God up to something in all this? Is it possible that the concern of the world over a problem that cannot be solved without massive return to responsibility and morality is God's platform for the Last Awakening? Is this a final stimulus He has engineered out of our ignorance and wrong for both evangelism and global missions at the critical edge of this next century?

The Final Emphasis for Revival

Perhaps this is the last and final significance of that word *salvation*. It is global in dimension. Are we called to help deliver the very creation around us from some of its suffering?

Every person who becomes a Christian takes some of the hurt not only from God's heart, but from the creation that agonizes with God. If you really want to heal the land, begin with the furrowing of your own heart and cry out to God for His mercy on our poor and broken creation.

If you have never done this before, make your peace first with God. Then you will have the grace, wisdom, and power you need to attempt a task that will never be solved by human effort, money, or technology alone. Following this chapter, in Appendix 1 (p. 181), is a small guide to help you do just this.

As Samuel Logan Brengle recorded the day after his life-changing meeting with God:

> I walked out on Boston Commons before breakfast, weeping and praising God. I saw a little worm wriggling on the path; I stepped over it. I didn't want to hurt any living thing. I loved the children; I loved the horses; I loved the dogs and the cats; I loved the heather—I loved the whole world![8]

And what a world it is! If you know the Author, the Books He wrote are so much more astonishing (Psalm 19:1; John 5:39). This is what I want you to do. The next time you come upon some lovely glimpse of God's glory in His creation, recall the dancing vision of Scripture: "All the trees of the field shall clap their hands" (Isaiah 55:12). I read that verse as a child of God, and now I understand why. With Him, you walk in a world full of wonder.

Making Peace
with Your Creator

The God of creation is real. Jesus Christ is alive! He loves you and is concerned for your well-being. He is the absolute Reality on which all truth is ultimately grounded. His message for you and your world is contained in the collection of 66 books called the Bible. Its transcendent teachings have stood the test of time, the scrutiny of scholars and the furnace of practical experience. They speak not only about history but how to live today in every level and facet of life.

The Bible's theme is God's plan of freedom from sin and death, a message that has delivered millions in every nation from self-destructive habits and given them a life both abundant and eternal. By first entering into and then developing a personal relationship with this living God, you will find everything you need for life on earth and for all eternity. Your life will have a sense of purpose marked by confidence and peace of mind. You will understand the true meaning of life. And God Himself will be your loving Father and your great Friend to give you power and guide your steps.

From the Bible we learn these facts:

1. God created humanity and nature for a wonderful purpose, but an act of rebellion and self-centeredness by the first man and woman caused our race to lose our relationship with Him and fall into the state of moral pollution called sin. Our sad legacy is now a nature wholly self-centered and impure in thought, word and deed. Our best efforts are selfish; apart from God we cannot even agree on what "good" is.

2. God's laws revealed in the Bible are not inventions, but *descriptions of reality.* They tell us truthfully how things are in the moral world. We do not actually "break" God's laws; they break us. We are punished *by* our sin as much as we are punished *for* our sin. All true law has a penalty as important as the law it is designed to protect. The penalty for sin, the violation of God's moral law, is *endless death* and *eternal separation from God.* If we live like hell here, our death will only confirm to us the reality of hell forever. Whether we consider our violations large or small, the sentence must be the same: The "wages of sin is death" and "the soul that sins shall die."

3. On our own we can do nothing to cancel or escape this sentence. We deserve to be judged. Nothing we can say or do can possibly justify the life we have lived and the things we have done to hurt ourselves, others, the creation around us and, most of all, God.

4. But God has no personal problem with seeking to forgive and restore us. Even in our rebellion He has never stopped loving us nor seeking to pardon us. In fact, at great cost to Himself, God made a sacrifice to provide a way back to His heart and our true home.

5. In Jesus Christ God became a man and lived among us. He personified God's love, wisdom, power and compassion. Born like no man before Him, He lived a sinless life without historical equal, spoke in wisdom as no man ever

spoke, and demonstrated beyond contention divine power and love in His miracles of healing, provision and deliverance. He even raised three people from the dead. Then, to the astonishment of the world, He Himself rose from the grave.

6. What seemed at first tragedy turned out to be divine strategy. To liberate us from our death sentence and reconcile us to Himself, Jesus laid down His sinless life as a substitute for the penalty you and I so thoroughly deserve. He gave Himself as the ultimate sacrifice for our sin and made our forgiveness and pardon possible. Now if you will trust Him as your substitute, you can go free. The God-Man on the middle cross has taken your place!

7. After three days in the tomb Jesus *rose from the dead* by the power of His Father. He was seen by hundreds of witnesses, has been met since then by millions all over the world and lives today as the ultimate Victor over sin, death and the grave. Because of what Jesus did, anyone who believes Jesus Christ is God's Son and trusts in His complete work on the cross for pardon and cleansing will be forgiven of sin and restored to friendship with God. By His Holy Spirit, God Himself will enter your life and break the enslaving power of sin once and for all. The resurrection of Christ is divine testimony that the power of death, destruction and decay in our world can be arrested and broken forever.

8. You will not only be given the gift of eternal life to live forever with Him, but your life here and now will be forever different. You will be given a new set of spiritual eyes with which to see and help your world. You will be empowered by His Spirit to understand and implement real and lasting changes in every sphere of your actions and influence. But to experience this you must make a conscious decision to surrender your life to Jesus Christ as your Lord and Savior.

9. This experience is called the "new birth." God tells us in the Bible that the only way a person can become a true Christian is to be "born again." The essential conditions for receiving this new life in Jesus are:

   a. **Honesty:** All your life you have been living a lie. When you come to God, you must face for the first time the truth about your sin. To do this you must be *utterly real.* God will not do business with people who do not mean business with Him. "He that covereth his sins shall not prosper: but whoso confesseth and forsaketh them shall have mercy" (Proverbs 28:13).

   b. **Repentance:** "I confess that I am a sinner and I cannot save myself from sin." True repentance means turning completely from your selfishness, with the determination to sin no more. Ask the Holy Spirit to help you *see, hate and forsake* your sin. True repentance means *giving up all rights to your life*; you must *die* to all your own plans, dreams and ambitions and put yourself into God's loving hands for whatever He wants of your life. True repentance also means being willing, as far as humanly possible, to *make right all known wrong.* Whatever the Holy Spirit speaks to you about, whether it is forgiveness of those who have hurt you, confession of wrong to another or restoring or repaying someone, the Lord Jesus will give you the courage and words to make it right.

   c. **Faith:** "I believe that God is real and that Jesus Christ is His Son. I freely confess that He died on the cross for the penalty I deserved. I believe that I can receive His forgiveness and a new life through the power of His Spirit living within me." This act of faith is neither and idea nor a feeling but *an intelligent and deliberate act of the will.* Give Him your doubts, your weakness and your loneliness. Your heart will never have peace, your doubts will never clear up, you will never die to the world until you trust, surrender, *believe* from your heart!

Why wait any longer? Jesus Christ by His Spirit is knocking at the door of your heart, waiting to come in. You can pray a simple, life-changing prayer right now.

In your own words *confess* to Him that you are a sinner and that you hate your sin. *Ask* him to forgive you and cleanse your soul from all that is not right. *Surrender* your life wholly to His mercy and power, and ask Him to take over total control of your life, now and forever. *Thank* Him for His forgiveness and ask Him to show you how to live for Him.

The Bible says,

> *If thou shalt confess with thy mouth the Lord Jesus,* and shalt *believe in thine heart* that God hath raised him from the dead, *thou shalt be saved.* For with the *heart* man believeth unto righteousness; and with the *mouth* confession is made unto salvation. . . . The same Lord over all is rich unto all that call upon him. For whosoever shall call upon the name of the Lord shall be saved.
>
> Romans 10:9–13 (italics added)

What He has done for countless men and women around the world, He can and will do for you. Just ask. And join us to help love His world in the adventure that never ends!

Romans 8:18–23: Window to God's World

What is the focus of nature on this planet? Does it have any sense of future? Does it possess in any sense its own subhuman dream?

The Bible treats the creation as if it *does* in some way have a deliberate purpose as a system. Six verses from the apostle Paul about the creation are critically important in understanding this purpose. In this section, I would like to present a succession of comments on and interpretations of these verses.

"Irrational" Creation Waits

Amplified in a late nineteenth-century translation, it reads like this:

> What though the path to that glory lies through suffering? The suffering and glory alike are parts of a great cosmical movement, in which the irrational creature joins with man. As it shared the results of his fall, so also will it share in his redemption. Its pangs are pangs of a new birth.

What of that? For the sufferings which we have to undergo in this phase of our career I count not worth a thought in view of that dazzling splendor which will one day break through the clouds and dawn upon us. For the sons of God will stand forth revealed in the glories of their bright inheritance. And for that consummation, not they alone but *the whole irrational creation, both animate and inanimate, waits with eager longing,* like spectators straining forward over the ropes to catch the first glimpse of the triumphant pageant.

The future and not the present must satisfy its aspirations. For ages ago, creation was condemned to have its energies marred and frustrated. And that by no act of its own; it was God who fixed this doom upon it, but with the hope that as it has been enthralled to death and decay by the fall of man, so too the creation shall share in the free and glorious existence of God's emancipated children. It is like the pangs of a woman in childbirth. This universal frame feels up to this moment the throes of travail—feels them in every part, and cries out in its pain. But where there is travail there must needs also be a birth.

Our own experience points to the same conclusion. True that in those workings of the Spirit, the charismata with which we are endowed, we Christians already possess a foretaste of good things to come. But that very foretaste makes us long— anxiously and painfully long—for the final recognition of our sonship. We desire to see these bodies of ours delivered from the evils that beset them and transfigured into glory.[1]

Romans 8:18–23 (italics added)

It Longs Eagerly

The King James Version translates the italicized phrase above like this: *The earnest expectation* [or *apokaradokia*] *of the creation* (verse 19). The phrase is used only twice in the Bible, here and in Philippians 1:20, where it is translated as Paul's "desire to depart, and be with Christ; which is far better."

"It denotes," wrote Albert Barnes in *Minor Prophets*, "a state of earnest desire to see any object when the head is thrust forward; an intense anxiety; an ardent wish." Two other meanings mentioned in *A Translator's Handbook on Romans* are that of "eager longing" and "desire with a rapidly beating heart."[2]

The text is even more specific—that creation as a system seems to expect its deliverance, now sadly appearing somewhat remote, from its Maker.

The verb for *longs for*, says Godet,

> is no less remarkable. . . . It comes from a simple verb *to receive* and two prepositions: *ek*, out of the hands of, and *apo*, from, from afar; so "to receive something from the hands of one who extends it to you from afar." This...vividly describes the attitude of the suffering creation, which in its entirety turns as it were an impatient look to the expected future.[3]

A Ruined Temple

It is as if creation itself (as we discussed in chapter 11), and not just men and women, experiences dislocation, lostness, being cut off. Erich Sauer writes eloquently of this disharmony and confusion:

> The material object of the temptation [of Eve] was taken from the plant kingdom, the instrument of the tempter from the animal kingdom. Therefore, on account of man, both of these realms, vegetable and animal, remain under the curse (Gen. 3:17), and the creation (which through man should have advanced to redemption and perfection) remains until now subject to vanity.
>
> Thus creation presents today that mysterious hybrid disharmonious condition, which in its conflict between happiness and unhappiness, wisdom and absurdity, purposeful adaption and confusion seems to render equally impossible both faith in God and denial of God. The world is so beautiful that for a time we can forget God and our guilt before Him, and the world is so terrible that we might on this account often despair of God.
>
> The world speaks to us as a revelation of God; it also stands rigidly before us as a riddle of God. Hence also the discord in the common human experience of nature and man's waver-

ing between glorifying nature and despising it, between happiness in nature and alienation from it, between worship of nature and treating it with contempt. . . . Jubilation and lamentation, kindness and cruelty, the joy of life and the grief of death—this all now convulses the whole world organism. At present nature is like a sublime temple in a ruined condition whose deeply significant inscriptions have been maliciously caricatured by a hostile hand.[4]

Nature's Dream

The whole creation groaneth and travaileth in pain together until now (verse 22).

We can, of course, write off this phrase as metaphor. But it is plain from the text that the promises made to man are to be expected as literal; and these same promises are made to the creation.

This is plainly not just mankind. The word *creation* refers to the entire created order (NAB, *the whole created world*; JB, *the whole creation*; NEB, *the created universe*), so the TEV renders this word by *all of creation*. In translating *all of creation*, it is important to avoid merely designating *all the people who have been created*, since the Greek text refers to the entire created universe. In some languages the closest equivalent is *everything that God has created*.[5]

As the creation was plunged into the Fall by no fault of its own, but by the stupid, selfish act of its appointed manager (suffering terribly as a consequence), so it appears to expect future freedom by the mercy of Another in an act of great power.

All of nature cries out to God for salvation, and

. . . In that day, I will hear, saith the Lord, I will hear the heavens, and they shall hear the earth; and the earth shall hear the corn, and the wine, and the oil; and they shall hear Jezreel.

Hosea 2:21–22

"God Shall Sow"

Israel here is called Jezreel, the name of one of the prophet Hosea's three children. Their names conveyed both the sentence and repeal of judgment on the land. The name *Jezreel* combines the memory of former punishment and future mercy. God had said, "I will scatter," but now, turning His chastisement into mercy to those who believed in Him, He changes the meaning of the word to "God shall sow." Israel in her dispersion, when converted to God, became everywhere the preacher of Him whom she had persecuted.

Of this Old Testament passage Barnes commented:

> As all nature is closed and would refuse her office to those who would rebel against her God, so when He has withdrawn the curse and [she] is reconciled to man, all shall combine together for man's good and by a kind of harmony all parts thereof join their ministries for the service of those who are at unity with Him. As an image of love, all from the lowest to the highest are bound together, each depending on the ministry of that beyond it and the highest on God.
>
> At each link the chain might have been broken; but God, Who knit their services together and had before withheld the rain and made the earth barren and laid waste the trees, now made each to supply the other and led the thoughts of men through the course of cause and effect up to Himself Who ever causes all which comes to pass.
>
> The immediate want of His people was the corn, wine and oil; these needed the fruitfulness of the earth; the earth by its parched surface and gaping clefts seems to crave the rain from heaven; the rain could not fall without the will of God. So all are pictured in a state of expectancy until God gave the word and His will ran through the whole course of secondary causes and accomplished what man prayed to Him for.[6]

What Happened to Creation?

Sanday and Headlam amplified Romans 8:20 like this:

The very creation on account of the sin of man has been subjected to the curse and has become "vain" or useless in regard to its original design, having been made subservient to the [now] evil purposes and passions of men.

And here is their commentary:

What does it mean that creation became "worthless"? Worthless as a concept means something "made with no meaning": no use, no purpose, full of nothing (empty) or "to be as though it were nothing." The verb rendered *condemned* is in the aorist tense, and literally means "made subject to," as a soldier ordered into his place. Some see here a specific reference to Gen. 3:17 when God brought His judgment against the earth because of Adam's sin. . . . Violence is imposed, as it were, on external nature.

[Yet] one may translate the last clause of verse 20 as "Nevertheless, God had this hope" or "God looked forward in confidence." This tragedy shall not continue. There is hope in the heart of the subject world that it shall be delivered from this bondage and participate in the liberty of the children of God. This representation may seem strange and unusual, but "we know," certainly adds the Apostle, that it is so; "the whole creation groans and travails in pain throughout every part."

Did the Early Church share then in this understanding of a morally linked creation? "For we know" seems to imply a fact of common knowledge to which the Apostle appeals, though the apprehension of it "may not have been so common as he assumes."[7]

Nature's Birth Pains

I said in chapter 11 that I sometimes wonder if the convulsions of nature in disasters like earthquakes, eruptions and floods are the ugly parables of her private pain. Listen again to the amplification of Romans 8:

. . . The creation shall share in the free and glorious existence of God's emancipated children. It is like the pangs of a woman in childbirth. This universal frame feels up to this moment the throes of travail—feels them in every part, and cries out in its pain. But where there is travail there must needs also be a birth.

To the numbed victims of a killer quake it sometimes seems that Satan himself has a hand in the senseless death and in the destruction of life and property. As the thief who comes "to steal, and to kill, and to destroy" (John 10:10), he is referred to—figuratively, at least—as "the man that made the earth to tremble, that did shake kingdoms; that made the world as a wilderness, and destroyed the cities thereof" (Isaiah 14:16–17).

But the Bible also attributes at least some of the earth's violent convulsions to the direct judgment of God. Referred to as a "new thing," the earth opened her mouth and swallowed the rebel sons of Korah (Numbers 16:30–34), an act referred to in awe elsewhere in Scripture (Deuteronomy 11:6; Psalm 106:17; Jude 11).

Volcanoes erupting and the earth shaking are metaphors of the visit of a holy God in anger (Judges 5:4; 2 Samuel 22:8; Psalm 46:2-3; 77:18; 104:32; 114:7). I can testify personally that there is nothing in all the world so deeply unsettling as the feeling you get from the unheard subsonic vibrations that precede and persist after a major earthquake or eruption. No wonder the first thing many people think of when one happens is the judgment of God!

None of this is the focus here. Scripture reveals that nature's greatest pain, like that of a woman in childbirth, is not its *past* hurt, but the *present* prolonged agony of waiting for something deeply wanted—promised relief in the coming of a new creation.

The phrase used here, *travails in pain* (*sunodino*), comes from two words meaning literally to have parturition pains (the extreme pains of childbirth) "in company with" (in concert, simultaneously)—that is, to sympathize (in expectation of relief from suffering). Explained Barnes:

> It denotes any intense agony or extreme suffering; it means here that the condition of all things has been that of intense,

united and continued suffering; in other words, that we are in a world of misery and death.[8]

Redemption

The suffering is necessary; something beautiful is going to be born.

From *A Translator's Handbook on Romans*:

Creation itself would one day be set free from its slavery to decay and share the glorious freedom of the children of God. . . . "Glorious freedom" may be rendered "to be set free in a wonderful way" or "will be given the wonderful liberty." But not just creation alone; we who have the Spirit as the first of God's gifts, we also groan within ourselves as we wait for God to make us His sons and set our whole being free.

A literal translation of the phrase "the Spirit as the first of God's gifts" (firstfruits) is not easy because it introduces a technical Jewish term . . . taken from the sacrificial system; it describes the first yield of the harvest or the first offering of animals which had to be dedicated to God before the rest could be used. In the present context, the word is used of that which God gives man, rather than that which man offers to God, and so the imagery is changed somewhat. . . . There are passages also where this term appears to be the equivalent of another Greek word, *arrabon*, with the meaning of a "guarantee" or "promise" of something to come (so I Cor. 15:20). . . . Moffat and Goodspeed follow the same interpretation and also retain something of the imagery: "a foretaste of the future."[9]

And finally, from Godet's *Commentary on Romans*:

"Until now"—even after redemption is already accomplished. The renovating principle has transformed the domain of the Spirit; for it became penetrated therewith at Pentecost. But the domain of nature has remained till now outside of its action. It is in this respect with the whole as with the individual.[10]

Agriculture and Moses

by Charles Lynn[1]

If it was for sins that man was condemned to till the ground, it was the most merciful judgment that almighty Benignity could have inflicted on him.

Daniel Webster at the
New York Agricultural Society

Laws About Wealth

The Hebrew constitution made sure the poor would not be victims of the rich and powerful. Through the agrarian reform laws of Moses, poverty and riches were impossible. These land laws made virtue of individual independence and had built-in deterrents to the greed that modern civilization has experienced. This greed causes nations to look at other ideologies to remedy their legitimate needs for reform from oppressive land ownership. Under God's law a few could not hold the wealth.

Moses' creed gave land labor dignity and assured workers of the field their rights and protection from unjust landowners.

The rich simply could not accumulate all the land because no lease could run beyond fifty years.

Justice

To assure this administration of equity, local magistrates were elected by the people. These magistrates were of utmost importance to implement the God-given laws of judicious land ownership.

The Hebrews were commanded to

> Take you wise men, and understanding, and known among your tribes, and I will make them rulers over you.
> Deuteronomy 1:13

These were to be able men who feared God, truthful men who hated covetousness. Moses sought four qualifications in these civil rulers: ability, integrity, fidelity and purity. They were to assure the tillers of the land that justice was at hand and that any complaint or violation of land laws could be heard in a court system.

The delay of law, furthermore, was unheard of. Courts of various grades were established, from town courts to high courts of appeals. There were rulers over thousands, rulers over hundreds, rulers over fifties and rulers over tens to judge the people (Deuteronomy 1:15). Under such a system a proletariat class was avoided, for the whole court system was created to hear the voice and needs of the land workers.

No Standing Army

Another benefit in Moses' agrarian plan was peace: The original Hebrew constitution made no provision for a standing army. Citizens held their land on condition of military service when required, thus forming a national defense for which no soldiers were paid.

The intense agricultural character of the Hebrews made for a peaceful life in which people could eat the fruit of their labor without fear of exploitation from their fellows. It was God's intention to marry the people to the land and keep them from war and the temptation to start wars.

War destroys land and fields and disrupts harvests. Light and darkness are closer to one another than land husbandry and war. (Ancient German leaders distributed land annually in their country in order to divert the thoughts of the people from war to agriculture.)

No Cavalry

To make His chosen a passive people on earth, God prohibited Israel from using a cavalry. Joshua was directed to hamstring the horses of defeated enemies. This practice was followed as late as King David's reign. The fact that Moses forbade a superior cavalry is proof that God designed His people for peace, not military glory that was the norm for nations of the day.

Negotiation First

Often the Hebrews had to fight against nations that had chariotry and other instruments of iron superior to the weaponry of the land workers of Israel. The way prescribed for God's people was an effort at peaceful negotiation (see Deuteronomy 20:10–12).

According to Josephus, it was required (except in the cases of the Canaanite nations) that prior to battle a herald be sent to the enemy with proposals of peace, and not until talk had failed was force called upon.

Festivals

A stronger proof of God's design for peace for His people was the law of festivals. Three times a year all males were required to go to the capital. It would have been hard to scheme and execute a foreign conquest when the men had to go so often to a festival. Intrusions into other countries could take months and sometimes years, and then only in the springtime when the kings went out to war.

Some Hebrew scholars believe that David's sin in numbering the people included the motive of aspiring to establish a great martial government. Thus, having his mind filled with the spirit of conquest that motivated other rulers of his day, David (in these scholars' view) became *common* and no longer heeded his own words: "I am for peace: but . . . they are for war" (Psalm 120:7). He had lost patience with God's way. The spirit of conquest had consumed him.

Plunder

Most kings of Moses' day plundered at conquest. In contrast, Moses was not a conqueror but the meekest man on earth (Numbers 12:3). He was commanded by God to ask permission to march through other nations, promise to abstain from treading down the fields and pay for everything he consumed. God himself honored the fields of men.

Moses was a humble man who saw how shallow martial glory was in a day when men's delight was to conquer. He saw that *the greatness of a nation does not rest in its great armies or uncounted acres of recovered booty, but in virtues of land industry and the triumph of wisdom.*

The Best Foundation

The doctrine that agriculture constitutes the best foundation for propriety and the happiness of a republic is the tenth principle of Moses', realpolitik. He labored to sketch in the people's minds the image that their country was best adapted to agriculture. He said it was a land flowing with milk and honey, with brooks of water and fountains. It was a land that received rainfall (drank the river of heaven). It included a culture of vineyards and olive gardens.

Moses made provision in their constitution that *no Israelite could be born who did not inherit a piece of land.* Thus, *the greatest pursuit of man was the pursuit of agriculture.*

Relation to Science

The slightest deviation in nature—rainfall, snowfall, dew or wind—affects the farmer, and God controls them all. The relation of science to agriculture is vital. To think of agriculture as unscientific is false and not biblical. To refuse to apply science and supplements to the land would be as neanderthalic as not taking a vitamin to supplement our natural bodies. Both the body and the land have been robbed from their divine state and need to be supplemented.

The nature of soil and plants and the special food they require is complex.

Farming is a science that must be mastered. There is no other pursuit in which so many laws of nature must be understood and consulted. To turn over the earth is to dig into the miracle of creation itself. As feeble human beings we must be reminded that our physical bodies will return to the earth. It is what we are made of.

Solomon had a God-given scientific mind. The Scripture says he had "largeness of mind like the sand on the seashore" (1 Kings 4:29, RSV).

> He spoke of trees, from the cedar that is in Lebanon to the hyssop that grows out of the wall; he spoke also of beasts, and of birds, and of reptiles, and of fish.
>
> 1 Kings 4:33

Solomon advanced agriculture to a scientific zenith in his day.

Honor

Only the most callous and undiscerning nations have reduced the tillers of soil to a peasant rank among their citizens. At one time in their history Greeks let only the slaves and dregs of the culture till the land. (The esteemed professions of Greece were wrestling and boxing.) This was hundreds of years before Western industrialization relegated agriculture to a lower status.

Moses sought to make agriculture the channel of Hebrew industry. He *honored* the employments of agriculture. Men passed from labor in the fields to public office and back to the fields.

The prophetic reformer Elisha was plowing when God called him. Amos was called from working among the sycamore trees. Men who worked the land were considered more fit to rule over the common people than the "white collars" who practiced other trades.

Land Ownership

History wears a dark cloak, and its pockets are full of periods when certain individuals held an unrighteous monopoly of the soil, making *many* the slaves of a *few*. Nearly all the political evils that have afflicted mankind have resulted from this unrighteous monopoly. History shows that improper land proprietorship is a scourge to any people.

The earth must be owned by those who till it! Ground is a gift to mankind for his survival.

Under Rome, Curius Dentatus once told his soldiers who insisted on a larger division of land of conquered nations, "God forbid that a citizen should look upon that as a small piece of ground, when it is sufficient to support a man."

Patriotism

Agriculture strengthens the love of country. Most Americans have no idea of the deep bond between land and mankind. The heart of a husbandman is bound to his field. His affections are higher to his land due to the sacrifice spent on the soil and the fact that in most cases his land came from a long line of time-honored ancestors. Loyalists in a country are usually rural dwellers. When land is severed through exploitation, war or greed, our source of life is cut asunder.

In the womb a human being is ordained to live by an umbilical cord. *But once outside the womb he or she is to live by a new cord, the land, and not have this new cord severed.*

Patriotism is a blind impulse if it is not founded on a knowledge of the blessings we are called upon to secure and the privileges we defend.

Relation to Foreign Commerce

Moses so bestowed dignity on land labor that he seemed indifferent to foreign and maritime commerce. Great Britain, Holland and the U.S., by contrast, acquired most of their wealth through foreign trade. We are bordering on economic woe from such policy today. Foreign countries have buffeted our economy through imports. In 1842 the annual Indian corn crop from Tennessee and Kentucky was worth as much as all our exports to England or France.

In foreign trade, while individual man rises, multitudes sink. While land labor is rural and quiet, buying and selling are the chief industries of busy cities. The giving and receiving of wages on an hourly basis often produces a collision of interests, while in agriculture the man or woman who owns acreage stands side by side in esteem and friendship with his or her colleagues.

Further reasons why Moses could have discouraged non-agricultural commerce:

⇥ Commerce would tend to lead the Israelites to develop *compromises by contact with the idols of foreign nations,* which could draw them into idolatry.

⇥ Industrialization could entice many people to leave their country and settle in foreign lands, *weakening their relations to home and patriotism.* A true hard-core merchant is an international person who may easily lack interest in or affection for his own country, interested mainly in what brings him capital gain.

⇥ It could introduce *tastes and luxuries that the nation could not afford to indulge in.*

⇥ If God's people had no ships, they would pose *no threat to the shipping trade.* With ships, the populations of Sidon and Tyre could get jealous over their loss of the market to the Hebrews. (France became the enemy of England and Holland over the East India Trading Company.)

Bad middle management over our agriculture can lead to non-productivity. Moses' prophetic eye was set to foresee such problems.

Solomon fell prey to a diverse extended economy. He had many harbors and laid his territories over a large area. He built Tamor in the desert as a station for caravans. The flow of wealth through numerous industries ruined the country and made Solomon's family "international."

Religious men learned to hate commerce and at times over-reacted. In the year 1090 Pope Urban II decreed that it was not possible to have a good conscience and do the trading of a merchant. Claudian law forbade senators to have any ship at sea that held more than forty bushels. Only agriculture was considered honorable for a Christian.

Yet today most religious institutions have contributed to injustice in landownership rather than presenting the biblical mandate to correct the injustice.

Other Industry

Were God's people to survive only on an agricultural-based economy? No. Industry should not be suppressed or limited to agriculture. Under the Hebrew government, commerce and industry had their part.

The abundance of industry was illustrated by the fact that Israelites were able to build the Tabernacle, intricate and requiring detail in skill and material. They made cloth of wool, cotton, goat hair and silk. Some were professionals skilled in the art of dyeing by obtaining colors from vegetables. There were potteries, foundries, precious metalworks, inlaying and molding.

Later, as history progressed, Solomon's gardens, ivory, species of plants and splendid instruments proved that an agricultural society is a modern society. (Amos and Isaiah chronicled their complaint that the nation was seeking luxury. The daughters of Zion had more than twenty toiletry articles, mentioned in Isaiah 3:18–23.)

Many of the families taken to Babylon were workers in wood and metals. The poor were left to till the ground.

International commerce and provision for trading were made through the national festivals at which the entire male population was present.

Being located by the seas, God's people could enjoy maritime commerce benefits without engaging in them. Tyre and Sidon could provide them all they needed in exchange for agriculture goods. Caravans with non-domestic goods available for sale cut constantly through what is now the Jordan Valley on their way out of Africa to Persia and Arabia.

Those politicians of Israel's day who preached that each man should be content "under his vine and under his fig tree" (1 Kings 4:25) had the right spirit inspiring them.

Formula for National Productivity and Wholeness

God reveals His caring nature for people through Mosaic Law by instituting the privilege of having cultivated land and convenient lodging. Solomon echoed Moses' legislation when he said, "Prepare thy work without, and make it fit for thyself in the field; and afterwards build thine house" (Proverbs 24:27).

The whole scope of the Pentateuch, Israel's land guide, was to uphold the institutions of the family and property for inward productivity and wholeness as a nation. A political community could not be organized except on the basis of individual property and rights, administered judicially and maintained with divine prudence backing up the integrity of the land workers.

This formula is rare today among nations and often ignored by the Western and Eastern world cultures.

Appendix **4**

Agriculture through History

by Charles Lynn[1]

> The fields are laid waste,
> the ground mourns;
> because the grain is destroyed. . . .
>
> Joel 1:10, RSV

"By the sweat of your brow" is a good description of human toil and hardship in living by the land. From his first appearance on earth, mankind has worked as both a hunter and a farmer.

The farmers of ancient Israel faced great obstacles. Land was steep and arid; Israelis had to build terraces, carve out irrigation channels, dig water cisterns and hew rock oil presses to develop their agriculture.

Their Egyptian neighbors developed two modes of agriculture in response to the scorching heat and constant water shortage in the Nile Delta. One depended on the rainfall, the other on the Nile's periodic ebb and flow. In some eras farmers achieved

205

maximal results under these conditions and exported corn to ancient Greece and Rome. Initially Egypt was the granary of the whole civilized world, then Syria.

In Middle East mythology, pagan harvest holidays climaxed the yearly cycle. Holidays centered on the concept of the generative power of grain. To fill a granary was considered a blessing for the people, who sacrificed to the god of grain. Many of these rituals demonstrated their innate fear of hunger.

By the end of the Roman Empire, agriculture became highly specialized, assimilating the ancient knowledge of Egyptian, Babylonian and Hebrew farmers. Roman agricultural writings indicate a sophisticated understanding of cattle breeding and the development of new plant species.

Early Ecological Disaster

What happened to this advanced system of productive Middle East agriculture? It suffered a heavy blow during the seventh-century Arab conquest. After accepting Islam, the Arab tribes pursued a campaign of conquest and gradually swept through all the Middle East. When the Arab conquerors set fire to the great Library in Alexandria, Egypt, rare and important compendiums of agriculture, along with other treasures of science and literature, were lost forever.

The burning of this library marked a transition from an agriculturally productive era to one of devastation under Arab conquest and rule. It took hundreds of years to recover from these setbacks. Archaeological and historical research indicates their lasting damage to the coast of North Africa, the settlement of Carthage and the Numidian towns.

The same fate affected some of Iraq's major projects in the land of Two Rivers. Despite rampage, the agricultural achievements of the Abbasid Caliphate in Iraq still show this area's potential. Yet even at the height of this recovery period, Middle Eastern agriculture never again achieved the productivity or reached the zenith of its past.

People assumed for generations that a farmer producing enough food for his own needs was successful. Middle Eastern peasantry did at times produce surplus food they could barter or sell. But war, exploitation of resources and sudden, violent changes of government have disrupted their farming system and added to its backwardness.

When Napoleon campaigned in the Middle East, his conquest of Egypt and applied European technology brought socioeconomic changes. By the early 1800s, the Egypt of the original Mohammed Ali was eager to absorb European know-how and launched a statewide reorganization of land-use regulations. Ali's program introduced European expertise, along with a structure designed to extort more revenue from the peasants—and, of course, a new tax.

The Link Between Economics and the Land

There has been another problem in the decay of Middle East agriculture: the lack of a reasonable financing system. Without such a system, peasant farmers had to rely on ruthless moneylenders who charged exorbitant rates of interest on the money they loaned and became self-imposed partners. Omnipresent tax-collecting landlords and moneylenders gradually squeezed the peasant to nonproductivity and desolation.

Land tenure in the Middle East has been overshadowed by constant fear of ever-present tax-collectors, whether representing the local government, a religious order or an estate owner.

The prophet Amos denounced similar oppressive acts in ancient Israel, rebuking those cruel creditors who "impose heavy rent on the poor and exact a tribute of grain from them" (Amos 5:11, NASB). He scolded those who took the sandals of the poor as payment for debt (Amos 8:6). The herdsman from Tekoa also forewarned that they would face certain doom under such oppression, and that the land would "rise up like the Nile, and . . . be tossed about, and subside like the Nile of Egypt" (Amos 8:8).

In This Century

During the first decade of the twentieth century, Western colonial powers investing in the Middle East concentrated on export crops like cotton in Egypt and citrus and wheat in Syria and Palestine (at that time under British rule). Areas in North Africa under France's domain made great strides by applying French technology to North American climatic conditions. Since the farmers of the Middle East were no longer self-sufficient, governments in the region had to calculate carefully how much food they could afford to import. Amid this quandary of food shortage, the new Arab states were born in the 1940s and 1950s.

After World War II the Middle East increased its need for food imports from Australia, Canada, Western Europe and the United States. The situation also reflected the population explosion that occurred in the Middle East after World War II and the region's inability to cope with the problem of food production.

By the late 1970s Arab planners were overcome with a sense of growing power; their newly accumulated wealth of petrodollars suggested enormous capabilities once dormant but now ready to be activated. In 1979 Arab planners estimated an annual growth in grain production of 1.6% in the Middle East, reaching 17.3 million tons by the year 2000.

Yet this figure fell short of the projected need, approximately 36 million tons a year; and these estimates were made before the beginning of the extended drought that hit parts of Africa and the Middle East. The drought generated fears and a new cautiousness that affected the political outlooks of drought-stricken nations.

Morocco signed a treaty with Libya in August 1984, and at the same time requested wheat from the U.S. to cover her food demands. A dispute between the U.S. government and the shipping industry stopped wheat shipments to Morocco, Egypt, Iraq and Tunisia. Morocco saw this end in wheat shipments as a reprisal against her government for signing the treaty with Libya. Libya went ahead and gave Morocco a loan of $100 million at the beginning of 1985 to purchase grain. This ill-born treaty between Morocco and Libya was later terminated and Morocco returned to the open market for her needs.

> "Take up weeping and wailing for the mountains,
>   and a lamentation for the pastures of the wilderness,
> because they are laid waste so that no one passes through,
>   and the lowing of cattle is not heard."
>
> Jeremiah 9:10, RSV

Economists generally agree that when a nation is more than thirty percent dependent on food imports, the situation is dangerous. In 1960 Saudi Arabia imported 76% of her food, while Libya and Jordan imported almost 60%. This dependence on food imports created a sense of siege and insecurity among the Arab population, who began studying ways to become more self-sufficient.

A Very Expensive Solution

An extreme example of this push toward self-sufficiency was Saudi Arabia's decision to raise her own food despite a hostile climate and outrageous production costs. A wheat farm was built 350 miles from Riyadh, in the Ruba' al-Khali Desert. Land was leveled and irrigated with desalinated seawater from dozens of specially constructed installations. This massive farm investment yielded 55,000 tons of wheat its first year of production and 1.7 million tons the second. It covered all immediate Saudi needs for wheat.

In 1980 King Fahd of Saudi Arabia sent a gift of one hundred tons of wheat to Egyptian President Hosni Mubarak with a letter emphasizing the end of Saudi dependence on American grain supplies. (The gift was only a drop in the bucket and did not help Egypt's food shortage.) Saudi publications told the story of the nation's success.

But how much did it cost?

While the Saudis are reluctant to supply data, some Middle East spectators commenting on the price of this Saudi Arabian success compare it with the production price of Egyptian steel. At the Helwan factories near Cairo, a ton of Egyptian steel is forty times more expensive than a ton of steel from Pittsburgh, Pennsylvania. A bushel of Saudi wheat from Riyadh thus might cost four hundred times more than a bushel from Hutchinson, Kansas.

The extravagant Saudi Arabian wheat program is accepted by the poor and needy of the Middle East as another Saudi mirage, too costly to be realistic. It cannot solve the plight of Middle East hunger, but it can fuel hostility between the hungry and the well-fed.

Recent Efforts to Reclaim the Land

The early 1980s saw increased efforts by various Arab groups, such as the Arab Organization for Economic Development (AOED), to draw up plans for projected food production for the year 2000. AOED planners completed approximately 150 studies spanning all branches of agriculture, at a projected cost of $33 billion. But the studies were never implemented because of the sharp drop in oil prices. One high official in the AOED called the plans a "study in futility."

The year after the oil price drop was not encouraging for grandiose investments, despite the growing need for a breakthrough in the battle for an independent food supply.

There are other reasons as well why these long-range development programs did not work: distorted government statistics based on incomplete data from peasants, lack of machinery and skilled manpower, migration to urban centers and insufficient planning.

These conditions were reflected in Syria when they attempted to invest in the increase of agricultural products and raw materials in 1976. Syrian reports soon admitted that the situation was chaotic; they blamed the lack of education among the Syrian peasants and their refusal to accept new ideas.

These Syrian findings reflect a common Middle East pattern: Plans developed in the lofty offices of the Ministry of Agriculture end up in fiasco when implemented in the isolated countryside.

Food Shortages and Violence

In 1984 the Moroccan government decided to raise the price of bread and other staple foods. This decision sparked a series of demonstrations and riots throughout Morocco that left two hundred casualties. Today nearly half of Morocco's 21 million citizens live below the poverty line. The nation's foreign debt is almost $12 billion, about half of her gross national product. Official unemployment figures are at 20%, although in reality unemployment is much higher. Of the total population, 60% are under 25 and 75% are illiterate.

Roman history verifies that rioting mobs in the streets of Rome were calmed only with the news that corn boats from North Africa or Syria had arrived.

One of the first priorities of Middle East governments is to guarantee a food supply, whether produced at home or imported. More nations are trying to be self-sufficient, especially those who have suffered unrest due to this issue. But it is difficult for governments to plan ahead while standing on the shifting sands of Middle Eastern conditions.

Because Middle East nations are dependent on Western technology, Western planning must be used to solve the food crisis. The transplantation of Western know-how without Western hands-on involvement has in the past proved futile. Without technical advice, expensive equipment was abandoned and left in the fields to rust.

> All her people groan
>   as they search for bread;
> *they trade their treasures for food*
>   to revive their strength. . . .
>   Lamentations 1:11, RSV (italics added)

211

While political analysts and social scientists still assume that the flow of grain from Western to two-thirds world nations serves a humanitarian cause, it also creates a handicap by making receivers of this aid less self-sufficient. A way must be found to balance the great need of Middle Eastern and African nations for technical aid, and curb the desire of Western democracies to give away money, aid and staple food supplies to the needy.

The constant bottlenecks to food supply in Egypt and other Middle Eastern nations create alarming pressure every day on millions of people. There is a continual lack of dried peas, beans, rice, chicken and meat. Many people wait for hours to buy government-subsidized bread, only to arrive and find the shelves empty. Although this heavily subsidized food is kept very cheap (and items like cooking oil, flour, sugar and tea cost less than on the international market), politicians realize that maintaining these subsidies is disastrous to the economy. Egyptian Parliament member Saraj el-Din said, "Our social safety nets are a luxury we can hardly afford."

A Reason for Aggression

When food prices rise, special security forces go on high alert. There is direct correlation between a government announcement of a lifted subsidy and a strengthened machine gun position on a Cairo street.

Hidden hunger is another problem. Often food provided has sufficient bulk but insufficient calories. Research shows that sixty percent of Egyptian children suffer from disease caused by malnutrition. Opposition parties in Egypt now claim that two-thirds of the population suffer from hunger. In an attempt to assure their people of continued food supply, the Egyptian government changed the name of their Ministry of Agriculture to the Ministry of Agriculture and Food Security.

Food, like water, can provide a reason for aggression. When an economy grows but still fails to guarantee a food supply, when plans for restoring the desert are too expensive, and when the introduction of agricultural technology collides with backward populations, the use of violence makes sense to the disillusioned.

Algeria, Libya, Sudan, Iraq and Syria are watching Egypt carefully. Government leaders are balancing on a tightrope; they remember how food policies stirred bread riots even in seemingly stable Middle East governments.

Sadat went to war with Israel in 1973 because of the terrible state of the Egyptian economy. Later, at the peace conference at Jerusalem in 1977, he admitted that Egypt had had no alternative but to enter into battle. Their economy had been in such desperate straits that the government would soon have been unable to supply bread to the people. "I will not hide from you, my sons," said Sadat, "that at the time of our decision to go to war, we had reached a very difficult economic situation."

After the Six-Day War, Egypt received $500 million from Saudi Arabia and other Arab states to support her military efforts. The extra finances gave new life to the Egyptian economy. As the writer of Lamentations says, death by the sword is sometimes preferable to death by starvation:

> Happier were the victims of the sword
>   than the victims of hunger,
> who pined away, stricken
>   by want of the fruits of the field.
>   Lamentations 4:9, RSV

Peace — "And a little child shall lead them." — Isaiah 11:6

Topical Compendium of Scriptures on Ecology

Cursed Because of Sin

Unto Adam he said, Because thou hast hearkened unto the voice of thy wife, and hast eaten of the tree, of which I commanded thee, saying, Thou shalt not eat of it; cursed is the ground for thy sake; in sorrow shalt thou eat of it all the days of thy life; thorns also and thistles shall it bring forth to thee; and thou shalt eat the herb of the field.

Genesis 3:17–18

God said unto Noah, The end of all flesh is come before me; for the earth is filled with violence through them; and, behold, I will destroy them with the earth.

Genesis 6:13

The earth also is defiled under the inhabitants thereof; because they have transgressed the laws, changed the ordinance, broken the everlasting covenant.

Isaiah 24:5

Therefore hath the curse devoured the earth, and they that dwell therein are desolate: therefore the inhabitants of the earth are burned, and few men left.

Isaiah 24:6

The Consequences of Lost Dominion

I will not drive them out from before thee in one year; lest the land become desolate, and the beast of the field multiply against thee.

Exodus 23:29

The land is defiled: therefore I do visit the iniquity thereof upon it, and the land itself vomiteth out her inhabitants.

Leviticus 18:25

[Keep my statutes . . .] That the land spue not you out also, when ye defile it, as it spued out the nations that were before you.

Leviticus 18:28

Judgment Because of Sin

Your strength shall be spent in vain: for your land shall not yield her increase, neither shall the trees of the land yield their fruits.

Leviticus 26:20

I will bring the land into desolation: and your enemies which dwell therein shall be astonished at it.

Leviticus 26:32

Then the LORD's wrath be kindled against you, and he shut up the heaven, that there be no rain, and that the land yield not her fruit; and lest ye perish quickly from off the good land which the LORD giveth you.

Deuteronomy 11:17

All thy trees and fruit of thy land shall the locust consume.

Deuteronomy 28:42

. . . The land, unto which ye go to possess it, is an unclean land with the filthiness of the people of the lands, with their abominations, which have filled it from one end to another with their uncleanness.

Ezra 9:11

He called for a famine upon the land: he brake the whole staff of bread [*destroyed all their supplies of food,* NIV].

Psalm 105:16

The land is full of adulterers; for because of swearing the land mourneth; the pleasant places of the wilderness are dried up, and their course is evil, and their force is not right.

Jeremiah 23:10

I will make the land desolate, because they have committed a trespass, saith the Lord GOD.

Ezekiel 15:8

I called for a drought upon the land, and upon the mountains, and upon the corn, and upon the new wine, and upon the oil, and upon that which the ground bringeth forth, and upon men, and upon cattle, and upon all the labor of the hands.

Haggai 1:11

The nations were angry, and thy wrath is come, and the time of the dead, that they should be judged, and that thou shouldest give reward unto thy servants the prophets, and to the saints, and them that fear thy name, small and great; and shouldest destroy them which destroy the earth.

Revelation 11:18

Creatures Suffer Because of Mankind's Sin

Yea, the hind also calved in the field, and forsook it, because there was no grass. And the wild asses did stand in the high places, they snuffed up the wind like dragons; their eyes did fail, because there was no grass. O LORD . . . our iniquities testify against us. . . .

Jeremiah 14:5–7

217

... There is no truth, nor mercy, nor knowledge of God in the land. . . . Therefore shall the land mourn, and every one that dwelleth therein shall languish, with the beasts of the field, and with the fowls of heaven; yea, the fishes of the sea also shall be taken away.

Hosea 4:1, 3

How do the beasts groan! the herds of cattle are perplexed, because they have no pasture; yea, the flocks of sheep are made desolate.

Joel 1:18

We know that the whole creation groaneth and travaileth in pain together until now.

Romans 8:22

Land Cries Out to God

What hast thou done? the voice of thy brother's blood crieth unto me from the ground.

Genesis 4:10

If my land cry against me, or that the furrows likewise thereof complain . . . let thistles grow instead of wheat, and cockle instead of barley.

Job 31:38, 40

[They] shed innocent blood, even the blood of their sons and of their daughters, whom they sacrificed unto the idols of Canaan: and the land was polluted with blood.

Psalm 106:38

How long shall the land mourn, and the herbs of every field wither, for the wickedness of them that dwell therein? the beasts are consumed, and the birds; because they said, He shall not see our last end.

Jeremiah 12:4

They have made it desolate, and being desolate it mourneth unto me; the whole land is made desolate, because no man layeth it to heart.

Jeremiah 12:11

The field is wasted, the land mourneth; for the corn is wasted: the new wine is dried up, the oil languisheth.

Joel 1:10

". . . That upon you may come all the righteous blood shed upon the earth, from the blood of righteous Abel unto the blood of Zacharias son of Barachias, whom ye slew. . . ."

Matthew 23:35

The first angel sounded, and there followed hail and fire mingled with blood, and they were cast upon the earth: and the third part of trees was burnt up, and all green grass was burnt up.

Revelation 8:7

And there came out of the smoke locusts upon the earth: and unto them was given power, as the scorpions of the earth have power.

Revelation 9:3

And it was commanded them that they should not hurt the grass of the earth, neither any green thing, neither any tree; but only those men which have not the seal of God in their foreheads.

Revelation 9:4

Four Judgments of God on a Land

Son of man, when the land sinneth against me by trespassing grievously, then will I stretch out mine hand upon it, and will break the staff of the bread thereof, and will send famine upon it, and will cut off man and beast from it.

Ezekiel 14:13

If I cause noisome beasts to pass through the land, and they spoil it, so that it be desolate, that no man may pass through because of the beasts: though [Noah, Daniel and Job] were in it, as I live, saith the Lord GOD, they shall deliver neither sons nor daughters; they only shall be delivered, but the land shall be desolate.

Ezekiel 14:15–16

Or if I bring a sword upon that land, and say, Sword, go through the land; so that I cut off man and beast from it. . . .

Ezekiel 14:17

Or if I send a pestilence into that land, and pour out my fury upon it in blood, to cut off from it man and beast. . . .

Ezekiel 14:19

And I looked, and behold a pale horse: and his name that sat on him was Death, and Hell followed with him. And power was given unto them over the fourth part of the earth, to kill with sword, and with hunger, and with death, and with the beasts of the earth.

Revelation 6:8

Land to Be Given Rest, Like Its People

When ye shall come into the land, and shall have planted all manner of trees for food, then ye shall count the fruit thereof as uncircumcised: three years shall it be as uncircumcised unto you: it shall not be eaten of.

Leviticus 19:23

When ye reap the harvest of your land, thou shalt not make clean riddance of the corners of thy field when thou reapest [*Do not reap to the very edges of your field*, NIV], neither shalt thou gather any gleaning of thy harvest: thou shalt leave them unto the poor, and to the stranger: I am the LORD your God.

Leviticus 23:22

Speak unto the children of Israel, and say unto them, When ye come into the land which I give you, then shall the land keep a sabbath unto the LORD.

Leviticus 25:2

In the seventh year shall be a sabbath of rest unto the land, a sabbath for the LORD: thou shalt neither sow thy field, nor prune thy vineyard. That which groweth of its own accord of thy harvest thou shalt not reap, neither gather the grapes of thy vine undressed: for it is a year of rest unto the land.

Leviticus 25:4–5

Then shall the land enjoy her sabbaths, as long as it lieth desolate, and ye be in your enemies' land; even then shall the land rest, and enjoy her sabbaths.

Leviticus 26:34

Land Speaks of God and Reflects His Character

The land shall not be sold for ever: for the land is mine: for ye are strangers and sojourners with me.

Leviticus 25:23

The land, whither thou goest in to possess it, is not as the land of Egypt, from whence ye came out, where thou sowedst thy seed, and wateredst it with thy foot, as a garden of herbs: But the land, whither ye go to possess it, is a land of hills and valleys, and drinketh water of the rain of heaven: A land which the LORD thy God careth for: the eyes of the LORD thy God are always upon it, from the beginning of the year even unto the end of the year.

Deuteronomy 11:10–12

The LORD shall open unto thee his good treasure, the heaven to give the rain unto thy land in his season, and to bless all the work of thine hand: and thou shalt lend unto many nations, and thou shalt not borrow.

Deuteronomy 28:12

Ask now the beasts, and they shall teach thee; and the fowls of the air, and they shall tell thee: Or speak to the earth, and it shall teach thee: and the fishes of the sea shall declare unto thee.

Job 12:7–8

Land Is Blessed When People Are Righteous

Then I will give you rain in due season, and the land shall yield her increase, and the trees of the field shall yield their fruit. And your threshing shall reach unto the vintage, and the vintage shall reach unto the sowing time: and ye shall eat your bread to the full, and dwell in your land safely.

Leviticus 26:4–5

And I will give peace in the land, and ye shall lie down, and none shall make you afraid: and I will rid evil beasts out of the land, neither shall the sword go through your land.

Leviticus 26:6

Hear thou in heaven, and forgive the sin of thy servants, and of thy people Israel, that thou teach them the good way wherein they should walk, and give rain upon thy land, which thou hast given to thy people for an inheritance.

1 Kings 8:36

If there be in the land famine, if there be pestilence, blasting, mildew, locust, or if there be caterpillar; if their enemy besiege them in the land of their cities; whatsoever plague, whatsoever sickness there be . . . [hear thou].

1 Kings 8:37

If there be dearth in the land, if there be pestilence, if there be blasting, or mildew, locusts, or caterpillars; if their enemies besiege them in the cities of their land; whatsoever sore or whatsoever sickness [there be] . . . [hear thou].

2 Chronicles 6:28

If I shut up heaven that there be no rain, or if I command the locusts to devour the land, or if I send pestilence among my people.

2 Chronicles 7:13

If my people, which are called by my name, shall humble themselves, and pray, and seek my face, and turn from their wicked ways; then will I hear from heaven, and will forgive their sin, and will heal their land.

2 Chronicles 7:14

If ye be willing and obedient, ye shall eat the good of the land.

Isaiah 1:19

. . . Until the spirit be poured upon us from on high, and the wilderness be a fruitful field, and the fruitful field be counted for a forest.

Isaiah 32:15

I will make with them a covenant of peace, and will cause the evil beasts to cease out of the land: and they shall dwell safely in the wilderness, and sleep in the woods.

Ezekiel 34:25

And the tree of the field shall yield her fruit, and the earth shall yield her increase, and they shall be safe in their land, and shall know that I am the LORD, when I have broken the bands of their yoke, and delivered them out of the hand of those that served themselves of them.

Ezekiel 34:27

And they shall no more be a prey to the heathen, neither shall the beast of the land devour them; but they shall dwell safely, and none shall make them afraid.

Ezekiel 34:28

The earth which drinketh in the rain that cometh oft upon it, and bringeth forth herbs meet for them by whom it is dressed, receiveth blessing from God.

Hebrews 6:7

Lexicon Summary for Words Rendered *Land*

Following are words rendered *land* in the King James Version of the Bible—first, Old Testament words from the Hebrew, then New Testament words from the Greek. Accompanying each is the number of times each word appears in the Bible, its reference number in the Hebrew and Greek Dictionaries of *Strong's Exhaustive Concordance of the Bible*, the word itself, and a partial definition.

Old Testament Words for Land

Count	Strong's	Word	Partial Hebrew Definition
111	127	*adamh*	country, earth, ground, husband (man), (ry)
2	249	*ezrach*	bay, tree, (home-), born (in the land) of the
1315	776	*erets*	common, country, earth, field, ground, land
1	3004	*yabbashah*	dry (ground, land)
7	7704	*sadeh*	country, field, ground, land, soil, wild

New Testament Words for Land

Count	Strong's	Word	Partial Greek Definition
1	68	*agros*	country, farm, piece of ground, land
39	1093	*ge*	country, earth (-ly), ground, land, world
1	3584	*xeros*	dry, land, withered
3	5561	*chora*	coast, country, fields, ground, land, region
2	5564	*chorion*	field, land, parcel of ground, place, possession

Notes

Chapter 1

1. Isaac Watts, Volume 9, *Colonies Planted, Nations Blessed or Punished. Works of Isaac Watts: Psalms Paraphrased* (London: 1813), p. 101.

Chapter 2

1. Maleness is the target of feminist Goddess writers who collectively blame men for the rape of nature. This shows that men's first friendship was with nature before Eve.

2. Erich Saer, *The Dawn of World Redemption* (London: Paternoster, 1953), p. 71.

Chapter 4

1. Bertrand Russell, quoted by Colin Chapman, editor, *Christianity on Trial*, Book 1 (Oxford: Lion Publishing, 1974), p. 83.

2. A. C. Bhaktivedanta Swami Prabhupada, *The Nectar of Devotion* (Los Angeles: ISKON Books, 1970), p. 20.

3. Ibid., p. 22.

4. E. D. Buckner, A.M., M.D., Ph.D., *The Immortality of Animals and the Relation of Man as Guardian from a Biblical and Philosophical*

Notes

Hypothesis (Philadelphia: George W. Jacobs & Co., 1903), pp. 234–235.

5. Ibid.

6. Will Durant, *The Story of Civilization, Part I: Our Oriental Heritage* (New York: Simon & Schuster, 1935), p. 463.

7. Lynn White, "The Historical Roots of Our Ecological Crisis," *Science*, #155 (1967): pp. 1203–1207.

8. Ian L. McHarg, *Design with Nature* (New York: Doubleday, 1969), pp. 26, 197.

9. Ian L. McHarg (*Ontario Naturalist*, March 1973), quoted by John R. W. Stott in *Issues Facing Christians Today* (Basingstoke, Hants, U.K.: Marshall Pickering, 1984), p. 117.

10. Buckner, p. 236.

Chapter 5

1. George Greenstein, *The Symbiotic Universe* (New York: William Morrow, 1988), pp. 26–27, 68–97.

2. Hugh Ross, *Fingerprints of God: Reasons to Believe*, P.O. Box 5978, Pasadena, CA 91117.

Chapter 6

1. Arthur C. Custance, *Doorway Papers, Vol. III: Man and Adam in Christ* (Grand Rapids: Zondervan Publishing House, 1978), pp. 74–76.

2. David Barrett and Todd M. Johnson, "News from Around the World," *A.D. 2000 Global Monitor* (November 1990): p. 2.

3. Rick Lyman, "A Global Warning: More Land Turns into Desert as Fresh Water Is Squandered" (fourth in a series), *The Philadelphia Inquirer* (May 20, 1992): p. A12.

Chapter 7

1. Henry Drummond, *Natural Law in the Spiritual World* (London: Hodder & Stoughton, 1894), p. 274.

2. Charles Darwin, quoted by R. A. Millikan, *Evolution in Science and Religion* (New Haven: Yale University Press, 1927), p. 60.

3. Buckner, pp. 246–247.

4. Ibid., p. 248.

228

5. Charles Darwin, *The Origin of Species, Great Books,* 15th edition, Volume 49 (Chicago: Brittanica Publishers, 1978), p. 33.

6. Ibid.

7. Custance, pp. 52–74.

8. Darwin, p. 39.

9. Sadhu Sundar Singh, *The Spiritual Life: Pain and Suffering* (Madras, India: CLS, 1967), p. 21.

Chapter 8

1. Arnaldo Fortini, *Francis of Assisi* (New York: Crossroad, 1992), pp. 542–543.

2. Isaac Watts, *The Works of Isaac Watts: Psalms Paraphrased* (London: 1813), p. 328.

3. Buckner, p. 93.

4. Lance Lambert, *The Uniqueness of Israel* (East Sussex, England: Kingsway, 1982), p. 20.

5. Ibid.

6. Ibid., pp. 22–23.

7. Ibid., p. 25.

8. Ibid., p. 26.

9. Ibid.

10. Buckner, p. 12.

11. Ibid., pp. 62–63.

12. Ibid., p. 78.

13. Ibid., p. 79.

14. Ibid., pp. 80–81.

15. C. S. Lewis, *The Problem of Pain* (New York: Collins, 1957), p. 129.

16. Buckner, p. 92.

17. Gerard Manley Hopkins, "God's Grandeur," *The Norton Anthology of English Literature, Revised,* Vol. 2 (New York: W. W. Norton, 1968), p. 1433.

Chapter 9

1. Arthur W. Galston and Clifford L. Slayman, "The Not-So-Secret Life of Plants," *American Scientist,* Vol. 67, May-June 1979, pp. 334–37.

2. Loren Eisley, quoted by Dr. Paul Brandt and Philip Yancey in *Fearfully and Wonderfully Made* (Grand Rapids: Zondervan, 1980), pp. 55–56.

3. Cleve Backster, quoted by Thorn Bacon in "The Man Who Reads Nature's Secret Signals," *National Wildlife*, Vol. 7, No. 2, February–March 1969, pp. 4–8.

4. Alice Walker, *Everything Is a Human Being: Living by the Word* (San Diego: Harcourt Brace Jovanovich, 1988), p. 147.

5. *The Hebrew-Greek Study Bible* (Chattanooga: AMG International, 1984), p. 1648.

6. John Mbiti, *Christianity on Trial*, Book 1, Colin Chapman, editor (Oxford: Lion Publishing, 1974), p. 74.

7. Paulus Mar Gregorios, *Tending the Garden* (Grand Rapids: Eerdmans, 1990), p. 90.

Chapter 10

1. William H. Becker, "Ecological Sin," *Theology Today* (July 1992): p. 152.

2. Ibid., pp. 152–153.

3. Walter Brueggemann, *The Land: Overtures to Biblical Theology* (Philadelphia: Fortress Press, 1977), pp. 4–5.

4. Charles Lynn, unpublished manuscript (Grandview, Kans.: 1993).

5. Ibid.

6. Brueggemann, p. 54.

7. Brueggemann, p. 55.

8. *The Hebrew-Greek Study Bible*, p. 1675.

9. Becker, p. 160.

10. Ibid., p. 159.

11. Colin Brown, editor, *The Dictionary of New Testament Theology*, Vol. A–F (Grand Rapids: Zondervan, 1975), p. 518.

12. Ibid.

Chapter 11

1. Albert Barnes, *Minor Prophets*, Vol. 1 (Grand Rapids: Baker, 1978), p. 189.

2. Frederick Louis Godet, *Commentary on Romans* (Grand Rapids: Kregel, 1977), p. 317.

3. Merrill C. Tenney, ed., *Pictorial Encyclopedia of the Bible*, Vol. 4 (Grand Rapids, Zondervan, 1977), pp. 584–585.

4. Ibid., pp. 585–586.

5. Edith Schaeffer, *Hidden Art* (London: Norfolk Press, 1971), pp. 88–89.

6. Albert M. Wolters, *Creation Regained* (London: Intervarsity Fellowship, 1986), pp. 57–58.

7. *Electronic Encyclopedia*, Grolier Electronic Publishing, Inc., 1990.

8. Samuel Logan Brengle, *Portrait of a Prophet*, (Chicago: Salvation Army Supply, 1933) p. 52.

Appendix 2

1. William Sanday and Arthur Headlam, *International Critical Commentary: Romans* (Edinburgh: T&T Clark, 1902), pp. 204–205.

2. Newman and Nida, pp. 158–159.

3. Godet, p. 313.

4. Sauer, pp. 57–58.

5. Newman and Nida, p. 159.

6. Barnes, *Minor Prophets*, Vol. I (Grand Rapids: Baker Book House, 1978), p. 40.

7. Sanday and Headlam, p. 209.

8. Barnes, pp. 192–193.

9. Newman and Nida, p. 161.

10. Godet, pp. 315–316.

Appendix 3 and 4

1. Charles Lynn has traveled extensively over the last twelve years discussing ecological issues with agriculturalists, industrialists and world leaders throughout North America, Central America, Eastern Europe and the Middle East.

Bibliography

A.D. 2000 Global Monitor. David Barrett and Todd M. Johnson. November 1990.

Agriculture (unpublished manuscript). Charles Lynn. Grandview, KS: 1992.

All the Trees and Woody Plants of the Bible. David A. Anderson. Dallas: Word, 1979.

American Scientist, "The Not-So-Secret Life of Plants." Arthur W. Galston and Clifford L. Slayman. Vol. 67, May–June 1979.

And the Trees Clap Their Hands. Virginia Stem Owens. Grand Rapids: Eerdmans, 1983.

Answers to Prayer. Charles Finney. L. G. Parkhurst, Jr., ed. Minneapolis: Bethany, 1983.

Christianity on Trial, Book 1. Colin Chapman, ed. Oxford: Lion Publishing, 1974.

Christian History of the United States. Verna Hall and Rosalee Slater. San Francisco: F.A.C.E., 1975.

Commentary on Romans. Frederick Louis Godet. Grand Rapids: Kregel, 1977.

Creation Regained. Albert M. Wolters. London: Intervarsity Fellowship, 1986.

Dawn of World Redemption, The. Erich Sauer. London: Paternoster, 1953.

Design with Nature. Ian L. McHarg. New York: Doubleday, 1969.

Dictionary of New Testament Theology, Vol. A–F. Colin Brown, ed. Grand Rapids: Zondervan, 1975.

Did You Know? Pleasantville, NY: Reader's Digest, 1991.

Doorway Papers. Arthur C. Custance. Grand Rapids: Zondervan, 1978.

Earthkeeping in the Nineties. Loren Wilkinson, ed. Grand Rapids: Eerdmans, 1992.

Electro Technology Magazine, "Do Plants Feel Emotion?" G. de la Waar. April 1969.

Electronic Encyclopedia (TM). Grolier Electronic Publishing, 1990.

Popular Electronics, "Experimental Electroculture." George Lawrence. February 1971.

Popular Electronics, "More Experiments in Electroculture." George Lawrence. June 1971.

Electronics World. October 1969 and April 1970.

Everything Is a Human Being: Living by the Word. Alice Walker. San Diego: Harcourt Brace Jovanovich, 1988.

Evolution in Science and Religion. R. A. Millikan. New Haven: Yale University Press, 1927.

Francis of Assisi. Arnaldo Fortini. New York: Crossroad, 1992.

Fingerprint of God: Reasons to Believe. Dr. Hugh Ross. P.O. Box 5978, Pasadena, CA 91117.

Fearfully and Wonderfully Made. Dr. Paul Brand and Philip Yancey. Grand Rapids: Zondervan, 1980.

George Washington Carver. Basil Miller. Grand Rapids: Zondervan, 1943.

God and the New Physics. Paul Davies. New York: Simon & Schuster, 1983.

Hidden Art. Edith Schaeffer. London: Norfolk Press, 1971.

Immortality of Animals and the Relation of Man as Guardian from a Biblical and Philosophical Hypothesis. E. D. Buckner, A.M., M.D., Ph.D. Philadelphia: George W. Jacobs & Co., 1903.

International Critical Commentary: Romans. William Sanday and
Arthur Headlam. Edinburgh: T & T Clark, 1902.

Issues Facing Christians Today. John R. W. Stott. Basingstoke, Hants,
U.K.: Marshall Pickering, 1984.

The Land: Overtures to Biblical Theology. Walter Brueggemann.
Philadelphia: Fortress Press, 1977.

Minor Prophets, Vol. 1. Albert Barnes. Grand Rapids: Baker, 1978.

Moses and Agriculture (unpublished manuscript). Charles Lynn.
Grandview, KS: 1992.

Music of the Spheres. Guy Murchie Rider. London: Hutchison, 1967.

Natural Law in the Spiritual World. Henry Drummond. London:
Hodder & Stoughton, 1894.

National Wildlife, "The Man Who Reads Nature's Secret Signals."
Thorn Bacon. Vol. 7, No. 2, February–March 1969.

Origin of Species. Vol. 49, 15th edition. Charles Darwin. Chicago:
Great Books, Brittannica Publishers, 1978.

Panorama of Creation. Carl E. Baugh. Creation Evidences Museum
(Southwest Radio Church, Box 1144, Oklahoma City, OK
73101), 1989.

Philadelphia Inquirer, "A Global Warning: More Land Turns into
Desert as Fresh Water Is Squandered." Rick Lyman. May 20,
1992.

Pictorial Encyclopedia of the Bible, Vol. 4. Merrill C. Tenney, ed.
Grand Rapids: Zondervan, 1977.

Portrait of a Prophet. Samuel Logan Brengle. Chicago: Salvation
Army Supply, 1933.

Pollution and the Death of Man. Francis A. Schaeffer. London: Hodder & Stoughton, 1970.

Power of Prayer on Plants, The. The Rev. Franklin Loehr. New York:
Signet, 1959.

Problem of Pain, The. C. S. Lewis. New York: Collins, 1957.

Project Earth. William B. Badke. Portland: Multnomah, 1991.

Reasons to Believe. Dr. Hugh Ross. P.O. Box 5978, Pasadena, CA
91117.

Secret Life of Plants, The. Peter Tompkins and Christopher Bird.
Sydney, Australia: Penguin, Ltd., 1974.

Secret Powers of Plants, The. Brett L. Bolton. New York: Berkeley, 1964.

Science, "Historical Roots of Our Ecological Crisis." Lynn White. #155. 1967.

The Spiritual Life: Pain and Suffering. Sadhu Sundar Singh. Madras, India: CLS, 1967.

The Symbiotic Universe. George Greenstein. New York: William Morrow, 1988.

Supernature. Lyall Watson. London: Hodder & Stoughton, 1973.

Target Earth. Frank Kaleb Jansen, ed. Pasadena: Youth With A Mission/Global Mapping, 1989.

Tending the Garden. Wes Granberg Michaelson, ed. Grand Rapids: Eerdmans, 1987.

Theology Today, "Ecological Sin," William H. Becker. July 1992.

A Translator's Handbook on Romans. Newman and Eugene Nida. London: United Bible Society, 1973.

Uniqueness of Israel, The. Lance Lambert. Eastbourne, East Sussex, U.K.: Kingsway, 1982.

Works of Isaac Watts, The: Psalms Paraphrased. London: 1813.

For more information on this subject, write to:
Gordon Aeschliman
Christian Environmental Association
P.O. Box 25
Colfax, WA 99111